Praise for *MySpace Marketing: Creating a Social Network to Boom Your Business*

"*MySpace Marketing* is the quintessential low-down on guerilla marketing on the biggest social network on the planet. Marketers big and small need to learn how to connect with their target audiences via social media or get left in the dust. *MySpace Marketing* gives the grounding and the specific tips and traps essential for marketing success on MySpace."

—Mark Brooks, Editor, SocialNetworkingWatch.com

"An invaluable guide to the dos and don'ts of building and marketing to social networks— essential reading for the enterprise 2.0."

—Niall Cook, Author, *Enterprise 2.0: How Social Software Will Change the Future of Work*

"Social networking is the new PR and advertising—any business not starting to explore the online space will be left behind by the competition. *MySpace Marketing* gives a practical, step-by-step approach that any business can use for successful marketing on the popular site."

—Colleen Coplick, BuzzNetworker.com

"Social Networks like MySpace are critical to the future of marketing. With traditional tactics like advertising no longer effective, there is no better way to have prospects experience your brand."

—Paul Dunay, Global Director of Integrated Marketing, BearingPoint; Author, Buzz Marketing for Technology blog

"*MySpace Marketing* is a practical guide for anyone involved in brand building. From starting with strategy ('Is your business right for MySpace marketing?') to the ins and outs of profile creation and audience segmentation, this book is an essential primer for small business owners and large brands alike on one of the biggest social networks."

—Scott Monty, The Social Media Marketing Blog, Global Digital & Multimedia Communications Manager, Ford Motor Company

"*MySpace Marketing* takes a respectful look at the rich community of MySpace and instructs marketers on how to successfully become a part of that community. Part field-guide and part how-to manual, *MySpace Marketing* delivers a great read and solid advice."

—Kate Trgovac, Editor-in-Chief, OneDegree.ca

"I have read a lot of books on marketing on MySpace, but what makes *MySpace Marketing* stand out are the examples (mini case studies) of what actually works on MySpace. The examples of what type of marketing campaigns have been successful and what you can do to replicate that campaign are really insightful and provide me with enough information that I feel I could go and launch a successful marketing campaign on MySpace today."

—David Wilson, Social Media Blogger, http://social-media-optimization.com

"Social media marketing doesn't have to be a series of trials and errors. *MySpace Marketing* is one of the only resources I've seen that takes the guesswork out of how to market in one of the largest social networks. Regardless of level of experience or resources, it gives step-by-step strategies suitable for large and small companies alike."

—Lisa Braziel, Community Engagement Director, Ignite Social Media; Coauthor, *Social Media is a Cocktail Party*

MySpace® Marketing

Creating a Social Network to Boom Your Business

Sean Percival

800 East 96th Street, Indianapolis, Indiana 46240 USA

MySpace Marketing

ISBN-13: 978-0-789-73709-0
ISBN-10: 0-789-73709-4

Library of Congress Cataloging-in-Publication Data:

Percival, Sean.
  MySpace marketing : creating a social network to boom your business / Sean Percival.
    p. cm.
  ISBN 978-0-7897-3709-0
  1. MySpace.com. 2. Internet marketing. 3. Online social networks—Computer network resources. 4. Business enterprises—Computer network resources. 5. Web sites—Design. I. Title.
  HF5415.1265.P467 2009
  658.8'72—dc22
                            2008035326

Printed in the United States of America

First Printing: December 2008

Trademarks

Warning and Disclaimer

Bulk Sales

Que Publishing offers excellent discounts on this book when ordered in quantity for bulk purchases or special sales. For more information, please contact

U.S. Corporate and Government Sales
1-800-382-3419
corpsales@pearsontechgroup.com

For sales outside of the U.S., please contact

International Sales
international@pearson.com

Associate Publisher
Greg Wiegand

Acquisitions Editor
Michelle Newcomb

Development Editor
Kevin Howard

Managing Editor
Kristy Hart

Project Editor
Chelsey Marti

Copy Editor
Gayle Johnson
Water Crest Publishing

Senior Indexer
Cheryl Lenser

Proofreader
Language Logistics, LLC.

Technical Editor
Chris Caulder

Publishing Coordinator
Cindy Teeters

Interior and Cover Designer
Anne Jones

Compositor
Nonie Ratcliff

Contents at a Glance

Contents

About the Author

Sean Percival is a web developer and author with 10 years experience in e-commerce, web development, and Internet marketing. He is considered a social network expert and has been featured in *Forbes Magazine*, *The Orange County Register,* and several online publications. Sean lives in Los Angeles, CA, with his wife, Laurie.

Sean Percival's official website can be found at www.seanpercival.com.

Official Website for This Book

Join the official social network for *MySpace Marketing* at myspacemarketing.ning.com. Here you can network with other MySpace marketers and share your experiences. Updated information and techniques are also posted directly to this website.

Dedication

To my wife, for patiently dealing with so many late nights in social media land.

Acknowledgments

Thanks to my family and friends for their continued support and encouragement.

We Want to Hear from You!

As the reader of this book, *you* are our most important critic and commentator. We value your opinion and want to know what we're doing right, what we could do better, what areas you'd like to see us publish in, and any other words of wisdom you're willing to pass our way.

As an associate publisher for Que Publishing, I welcome your comments. You can email or write me directly to let me know what you did or didn't like about this book—as well as what we can do to make our books better.

Please note that I cannot help you with technical problems related to the topic of this book. We do have a User Services group, however, where I will forward specific technical questions related to the book.

When you write, please be sure to include this book's title and author as well as your name, email address, and phone number. I will carefully review your comments and share them with the author and editors who worked on the book.

Email: feedback@quepublishing.com

Mail: Greg Wiegand
         Associate Publisher
         Que Publishing
         800 East 96th Street
         Indianapolis, IN 46240 USA

Reader Services

Visit our website and register this book at informit.com/register for convenient access to any updates, downloads, or errata that might be available for this book.

Foreword

The Poetry of Social Networking to Court Customers and Invest in Relationships

In the era of the Social Web, everything we create and share online is open to public discovery, interpretation, and feedback. It introduces our thoughts, emotions, passions, and insights to new people and erases the geographic borders and boundaries that prevented us from artfully and naturally connecting with like-minded people around the world.

Your digital identity defines who you are. And in this genre of Web-savvy content creators and purveyors, your online reputation does indeed precede you.

Perception is reality.

The Social Web on websites like MySpace has effectively introduced us to a digital land rush that allows us to stake a claim to the markets where we can excel in ways previously impossible. We're creating and populating online societies and global neighborhoods where we can contribute to, and directly benefit from, the proliferation of innovation, interaction, and subsequent commerce.

It's nothing short of an incredible, life-changing opportunity for you to demonstrate the value, experience, and knowledge you represent to earn and invest in the relationships that propel your business as well as your professional and personal brand.

Maintaining a central presence online on social networks, in addition to a company website or blog, provides you with an effective dashboard for building strategic relationships with the very people in that network who can help your business grow.

A strategically developed profile on MySpace where your customers and are active provides you with a home base for presenting your value proposition, managing relationships, and also proactively engaging with prospects, consumers, and partners.

MySpace has evolved into a powerful, highly integrated platform, showcase, and resumé for your social capital—online and in the real world. A social profile facilitates presence aggregation, channeling all online activity through one main hub. Simply said, it becomes a repository for our ideas, expertise, differentiation, experience, and every social media object we create and share. This ultimately transitions from a static web profile into a dynamic and collaborative destination for the brand *you*.

In Social Media, your personal brand is defined by the sum of its distributed parts. Whether you realize it or not, your blog posts, comments on other blogs, updates on Twitter, and the pictures you upload, contribute to your online persona.

It's the curation of all our disparate pieces (social objects) online that collectively paint a picture of who we are, what we represent, as well as our strengths and weaknesses. This brand is yours to shape, cultivate, nurture, and craft.

We are living in a Social Economy and it is defined by the exchange of ideas and information both online and in the real world. The value and state of the exchange is indexed by the dividends earned through new opportunities and alliances. Relationships are the new currency of the Social Economy as they fuel and extend interaction, insight, and loyalty, and in turn, contribute to the social capital of the individuals who actively invest in their personal branding portfolio.

It's how we instill and create trust.

It's how we convincingly compel action through the demonstration of true expertise.

It's how we build a bridge between our business and our customers.

Social networks are living and breathing communities that are rich with culture and supported by the ecosystems that people create and depend upon for increased vibrancy, interaction, and value.

These digital cultures are not unlike the societies that define our world today. Technology changes, but people don't.

While social networks exist to connect us to others, just like in the real world, relationships are governed by strategic rules of engagement and natural human etiquette. Relationships are not earned nor will they bear fruit if they're simply relegated as cogs in your viral marketing machine.

Establishing an effective online presence and building rewarding relationships can only be accomplished by unbiased observation and genuine immersion.

The study of social sciences, such as anthropology and sociology, teach us to first observe the behavior, interaction, and culture of a society before we try to become a citizen, let alone market to it.

The profiles in social networks are so much more than avatars—this is something that's easy to forget. They're not target audiences for your messages and sales pitches. They are extensions and representations of real people and they are online to establish relationships that are mutually beneficial—just like you.

Instead of simply thinking about social networks as new ways to communicate with friends, family, and associates or sell captive constituents, let's instead view these communities as the headquarters for our online brand, collective expertise, and also the nerve center for connecting to our stakeholders.

Participation and interaction, outside of a sell cycle is the minimum ante for induction into the ecosystem.

Let's start by first answering these questions to effectively prepare us for a successful immersion into new online communities:

What do you stand for?

What are your intentions?

What value do you offer to the community?

Who are our customers and where do they go for information?

Why are our customers online?

What are the needs and real "pains" of those you're trying to reach?

How can you help, outside of selling something?

What will customers and peers say about their experience with you today and tomorrow?

It's important to weigh, factor, and proactively contribute to the impression you want others to have when they stumble upon or intentionally find your profile or how they perceive, react and respond to your initial and future contact. This is the first step in defining and shaping your online brand as we create a solid foundation for relationship building.

No matter what world you live in, we are all responsible for the public relations of any organization we represent. Everything we do, whether we're in PR or not, reflects on, and contributes to, the brand we represent.

Arming employees and our community with knowledge and expertise and empowering them to participate, creates an efficient, influential, and community-driven organization that stays in sync with stakeholders. It creates an active collective of influential voices who will help shape perception and provide help to those seeking advice. Instead of traditional top-down, us versus them marketing strategies, a relationship-powered approach commission the greater community to become an extension of your outbound activities, beliefs, knowledge, passions, and value propositions.

As marketing, communications, and service professionals with a heightened sense of social awareness and relevance, we earn the right to live and conduct business in the digital societies where we have invested in its maturation, education, and cultivation and the relationships that serve as its foundation and DNA.

We are both architects and builders who are creating the blueprints for and constructing the bridge that connects customers and the people who represent the companies they believe in.

To truly connect however, we must learn through listening to day-to-day online conversations related to our brand. This is the only way to honestly empathize with our customers—otherwise, we revert to common lip service.

We must observe the interaction and culture that connect the very people that contribute to a thriving community. We must become the customers we want to reach to genuinely engage with them. In the process we redefine sales, service, and marketing, by rebuilding our initiatives from a demographics-driven campaign to a more humanized approach—one that only inspires more meaningful activity, engagement, and results.

Building a bridge to our customers requires the humanization of our mission and our story.

It takes so much more than an understanding of the tools and technology that power social networks to inspire change and build long-term, meaningful relationships. It's our job, duty, and responsibility to reach our community, their way, and teach others to do so along with us, whether it's from within or externally.

It's one thing to be genuine, but it's altogether different to translate and effectively communicate what you epitomize to the various markets and what they're seeking.

Being human is far easier than humanizing your story.

Feel it.

Live it.

Breathe it.

Love it.

Embody it.

You are the personality and the soul of the brand you represent.

Actions speak louder than words and everything begins with listening. It is after all, the best listeners who serve as the best conversationalists. Listening reveals everything we need to know to effectively connect what we represent and what we know to the unique needs and questions of community participants. In the process, we become reliable and trusted resources.

Remember, people do business with people they respect and they continue to stay loyal because they trust the relationship with the people that represent the brand, not the brand in of itself.

In social networks and the all-encompassing Social Web, we earn the business and relationships we deserve. This is the poetry of social networking and relationship building.

MySpace is one of many popular social networks in a landscape which will only continue to evolve with the Web. But unlike other communities, MySpace has its own living and breathing ecosystem and thriving economy that attracts and congregates people and brands to actively engage with each other. It creates a veritable exchange that constructs an online second life that physically transcends into our real life.

MySpace is a thriving opportunity for small businesses, artists, and mainstream brands to connect with the very people who can not only become loyal customers, but those who we also empower and reward for establishing and extending online communities that carry our brands forward. MySpace is a rich and vibrant culture unto itself and rich with existing and potential brand ambassadors who can tell our story, even when we're not present to do so. All it takes is for us to first observe, identify, and listen to those people that we wish to engage. We then borrow from the science and lessons of anthropology and sociology to understand the behavior and dynamics that define the subcultures where we wish to participate. With an understanding of these digital societies and relevant psychographics fused with customer empathy and an adeptness for developing interpersonal relationships, we can adapt our value and story to transparently connect with tastemakers through genuine immersion.

Brian Solis is Principal of FutureWorks, an award-winning PR and New Media agency in Silicon Valley. He blogs at PR2.0, bub.blicio.us, and regularly contributes PR & tech insight to industry publications. Solis is among the original thought leaders who paved the way for Social Media. He's a cofounder of the Social Media Club, is an original member of the Media 2.0 Workgroup, and also contributes to the Social Media Collective. He is author of Putting the Public Back in Public Relations: How Social Media Is Reinventing the Aging Business of PR.

W e recognized from the beginning that we could create profiles for the bands and allow people to use the site any way they wanted to. We didn't stop people from promoting whatever they wanted to promote on MySpace. Some people have fun with it, and others try to get more business and sell stuff, like a makeup artist or a band, and we encourage them to do that."

Tom Anderson
MySpace cofounder

New Frontiers

Traditional advertising companies are very worried. Some of their most important demographics are not watching TV or reading magazines like they used to. Instead, you can find them online, spending the majority of their time navigating social networks like MySpace. These websites allow members to contribute, interact, and connect like never before. They forge new relationships, both personal and business-related. I guess you could say it's the modern-day equivalent of the diary, the local hangout spot, and the record store all rolled into one. On MySpace you can find a date for the weekend, a job, or even old classmates all in one visit. MySpace has been responsible for everything from marriages to divorces and even reuniting long-lost family members.

I Want MySpace, Not My MTV

Social network users spend, on average, 11 hours online per week, compared to 9.4 hours watching TV. Although heavy social network users still watch TV, 70% say their favorite time to spend online is during prime-time TV viewing hours.

Although the majority of its members use MySpace for communicating or online people-watching, thousands of businesses have also created their own pages for marketing purposes. This can take many forms, but the goal is pretty much the same in all cases: the more "friends" you have, the better. Befriending someone on MySpace can be compared to discovering a new business contact or lead. When you include these friends in your own social network, you are also creating a private advertising network at the same time. However, instead of the typical "shotgun blast" often found with traditional advertising, your social network now works like a net, allowing you to continually market to your ever-growing network.

Chances are you picked up this book because you already have experience with MySpace but you want to know more about its marketing potential. Perhaps you don't have experience and wonder what you're missing out on. Either way, this book will teach you some of my best secrets that I've used to help companies understand and monetize their promotions on MySpace. In the process, they created brand loyalty, received invaluable feedback, and had a great time doing it.

What Is MySpace Marketing?

MySpace was created primarily as a means for bands to promote their music to fans. It's no surprise that businesses noticed the potential and starting connecting with their "fans" as well. Today you find businesses of all types, from hairdressers to real estate agents, creating and marketing their own profiles on this massive network. In addition to multinational companies such as Adidas and Burger King, many small businesses have also embraced MySpace marketing to generate website traffic and leads. Converting this tangle of online human relationships into an effective promotional platform is what MySpace marketing is all about.

For the most part, marketing on MySpace can be broken into two types: paid advertisements and the more common method, which resembles guerilla marketing. Most companies take the latter approach, because running ads on MySpace can cost anywhere from $7,500 to $100,000 per month. This cost typically is out of reach for most companies, especially small businesses. Thankfully, MySpace marketing can work with any budget, because the majority of the promotion can be done for free. For companies with medium-sized budgets, you can also benefit from paid placements thanks to Google Adwords. We'll cover both, but I'm sure you're most interested in the free stuff, so there is a heavy focus on this.

The most important component of MySpace marketing is community. This is the key to MySpace's success and yours. Creating a community or social network around your promotion is a marketer's dream for many reasons. First, you get lasting brand recognition, because members will see your MySpace page several times through their normal usage. Second, you have the opportunity to capture visitors by joining them to your social network. This allows you to market to them repeatedly through various avenues on MySpace. Last, you are adding to the community just by being part of it and contributing. Marketing on MySpace is walking a fine line between advertising and personal relationships. In this book I'll show you how to take the first steps and continue to gain momentum.

Friending Is the New Advertising

In April 2007 an independent and comprehensive survey was performed to measure the impact that social networks have on marketing. The results were surprising, even to those who had already seen dramatic results firsthand. More than 40% of the 3,000 users questioned said they use social networks to learn more about a product. Additionally, 28% said they were referred to the product from an online friend, which adds great credibility to any promotion.

So what is all this talk about friends, and how do they relate to MySpace marketing? In a business sense, a friend on MySpace can be compared to a potential lead or existing customer. You gain friends by requesting friendship with other members and receiving incoming friend requests as well. It does come down to a popularity contest of sorts, where whoever has the most friends receives the most traffic. However, on MySpace, quality is usually better than quantity. Thanks to MySpace's rich demographics, it has no shortage of quality friends. It really doesn't matter what your promotion is for, because chances are your demographic already has members in the thousands, if not millions.

When we say "friending is the new advertising," we are confirming an emerging trend seen across the Internet. Surely you've noticed new features on some of your favorite websites that encourage you to join, contribute, and connect with other members. This is Web 2.0, and it is very social in nature. Millions of people are creating their own networks of both online and real-life friends in a truly engaging experience. Including your promotion in these networks gives you access to untold numbers of new connections.

Secrets of Success

With its army of 150 million users, MySpace currently holds the title of largest social network. In the annals of Internet history, few websites have experienced the sudden and explosive growth that MySpace has. When it comes to total traffic, MySpace is right up there with the big boys like Yahoo! and Google. At the time this book was written, MySpace was the fifth most popular website on the Internet.

MySpace also sees a staggering five million new user registrations each month. That's roughly equal to the population of Minnesota. This huge force of a website was founded in 2003 by Tom Anderson and Chris DeWolf and a very small team of programmers. How did these two unconventional executives create such a huge overnight success without a big marketing budget?

Their success can be attributed to a few things.

Good Timing

Friendster.com was actually the first to bring a social network to the masses in 2002, but it couldn't keep up with the demand. At the height of its popularity, Friendster.com could barely even serve web pages to visitors. Instead, visitors received lots of error messages as the servers tried to handle the huge surges of traffic. The MySpace founders were active members of Friendster.com, and they jumped at the chance to launch their own version. After just 10 days and probably unimaginable amounts of coffee, the first version of MySpace was launched. Although it had many bugs (and, let's be honest, it still does), this original framework and design are still used throughout MySpace.

Word of Mouth

To get the word out, MySpace held a company-wide contest to see who could sign up the most friends. Emails started to go out of the eUniverse offices in Los Angeles, and in a hyper-connected world, the invitations snowballed worldwide. Millions of frustrated Friendster.com users quickly jumped ship and in the process formed the largest online social network. The winner of the contest received $1,000. Not a bad investment, considering that MySpace was bought for $580 million two years later.

Precision Targeting

The first members invited to join MySpace were mostly photographers, artists, and other creative types. The founders knew that this passionate demographic would embrace the technology as a great way to showcase their work. Subsequent visitors found themselves inspired by this unique community and were eager to become part of it.

Leveraging Existing Contacts

At the time of MySpace's launch, its creator, eUniverse, owned CupidJunction.com, which had three million users. All these members were invited to join MySpace, giving the site a serious shot in the arm. eUniverse also advertised the launch on several other websites owned by the company.

Trust Your Users

Giving users almost complete freedom on MySpace empowered the very vocal and powerful Internet Generation. They took this freedom and ran with it when creating their own private space online. In the process they added "Fonzie" levels of cool to MySpace and brought all their real-world friends along with them.

The Future of Social Networks

These things are always hard to predict in an environment as dynamic as the Internet. However, the future of social networks has never looked better. Over the last few years they have continued to grow, with no signs of slowing. In addition to MySpace, an increasing number of other social networks are popping up, each offering its own twist on the popular medium. Although they have not reached MySpace levels of success, websites such as Facebook (www.facebook.com) and LinkedIn (www.linkedin.com) have also signed up millions of members and offer great online destinations. Companies have even started to include social networking features on their existing websites, hoping to turn passive visitors into contributing members.

Countless businesses such as YouTube and Photobucket offer services that piggyback on social networks, and they also have seen an amazing response. Photobucket was so successful that MySpace purchased it and plans to integrate its feature into MySpace. Some YouTube videos get more views than prime-time TV shows. YouTube owes its success to none other than MySpace, where the majority of its videos are posted. The social network of the future will be a mashup of several companies, each offering its own unique service.

Let's also not forget that the Internet Generation (people born between 1994 and 2001) has been the driving force behind MySpace. It's safe to assume that subsequent generations will embrace these technologies and take them to even higher levels. We can't discount the older generations, though. Recently they have started to join social networks in huge numbers and have even surpassed the high school kids who made MySpace so famous. Whatever the future holds, now is the time to capitalize and carve out some space for yourself or your business.

Welcome to MySpace

Is Your Business Right for MySpace Marketing

MySpace was initially created as a means for bands to promote their music to fans. It's no surprise that businesses and other promoters also noticed the potential of connecting with their "fans" as well. Today, you find business people of all types—from hair dressers to real estate agents—creating and marketing their own profiles on this massive network. In addition to multi-nationals like Adidas and Burger King, many small businesses have also embraced MySpace marketing to generate website traffic and leads. Converting this tangle of online human relationships into an effective promotional platform is what MySpace marketing is all about.

Essentially, marketing on MySpace can be broken down into two types: the first is paid advertisements; the second, more common method resembles guerilla marketing. Most companies take the latter approach because running ads on MySpace can cost anywhere from $7,500 to $100,000 per month. This cost is typically out of reach for most companies, and especially for small businesses. Thankfully, MySpace marketing can work with any budget because the majority of the promotion can be done for free. For companies with medium-sized budgets, you can also benefit from paid placements, thanks to Google Adwords. Both types of marketing are covered in this chapter, but I'm sure you're most interested in the free stuff, so there is a heavy focus on this.

The most important component of MySpace marketing is community. This is the key to MySpace's success and yours. Creating a community or social network around your promotion is a marketer's dream for many reasons. First, you get lasting brand recognition because members will see your MySpace page several times through their normal usage. Second, you have the opportunity to capture visitors by joining them to your social network. This allows you to market to them over and over through various avenues on MySpace. Last, you are adding to the community by just being part of it and contributing. Marketing on MySpace is walking a fine line between advertisement and personal relationships.

MySpace marketing is about having conversations. Ask yourself: Is this something people can have a conversation about? In traditional terms, this used to occur around the water cooler or perhaps at the neighborhood hangout. Today, however, these conversations take place on social networks like MySpace. Sometimes they occur publicly through message boards and blog posts and in other cases, behind private messages. Having a good presence on MySpace can help encourage these conversations to start. Think about what you will say, and through this book, learn how to participate the right way.

How Big Is MySpace?

Receiving somewhere between 30 and 70 million unique visitors each month, MySpace currently holds over 80% of all social network traffic. Users spend an average of around 200 minutes each day on the service. Engagement like this is not typical, nor are the amount of page views the website receives. Around 250,000 new users sign up each day, and over 100 million accounts in all have been created. In terms of traffic and reach, MySpace is HUGE.

Although the sheer number of MySpace users is great, the real value of marketing here is that you can target your key demographic so precisely. This way you don't waste time and effort promoting to those who aren't interested. MySpace has a diverse population. You would be hard-pressed to find a business that couldn't benefit from marketing through this new social medium. With so many users, even small niches find great benefit with MySpace marketing. Your promotion can now be distributed in a very filtered and granular fashion.

Although MySpace is well known for its army of 13-to-16-year-olds, in reality most of the site's users are older, with 87% over the age of 18. The younger crowd is great at clicking on web promotions but typically these clicks do not convert to online sales or leads. The 18-to-35-year-old demographic, however, is very comfortable with online shopping and has become the largest base of MySpace users. Regardless of what your age demographic is, you'll be able to find it on MySpace.

Understanding How Social Networks Like MySpace Work

At the heart of a social network are tools for communication and expression—two things that have become a huge force on the Internet in recent years. It's human nature to want to build relationships and express yourself, and websites like MySpace have given this power to millions. Many use these tools to keep tabs on real-life friends, but an increasing number of people are also using social networks to learn about products and create new personal (or business) connections. Although Internet message boards and online communities have been around for years, it took the advent of the social network to bring this concept to the masses. Currently, more than 240 million MySpace profiles have been created. This is a staggering number that shows no signs of slowing.

MySpace is only one of the thousands of social networks that now adorn the Internet landscape; other examples include Facebook, LinkedIn, and Bebo. There is even Dogster, which (naturally) is a social network for dogs. Its sister website is called Catster. Some offer unique twists on social media, but most keep to the same concepts of creating a profile, having friends, and establishing your own network. As connections between members are created, small networks within the larger social network begin to develop. New communities and relationships are developed, where information and ideas are shared.

A View of a Social Network

Social networks are made by a group of connecting profiles, sometimes referred to as "nodes." In MySpace's case, each node is an individual, a band, or one of the many other types of profiles. The way these nodes connect is what makes a social network such a valuable type of network. These connections are called several things, such as "six degrees of separation," "many to many," and "circle of friends." Friends, in fact, are the binding force of many of the networks. As shown in Figure 1.1, just one person can connect you to many others.

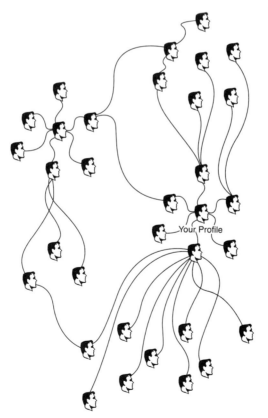

Figure 1.1
A single connection becomes many on a social network.

Here you can also begin to see some of the power of MySpace marketing. When you make just one new connection or friend, you are actually making many. Users view their "Friends" pages to see what their own friends are into. This gives your promotion the opportunity to be seen by new faces all the time. As I'm sure you can understand, the larger your friend network, the better. However, it's also important to maintain quality over quantity. Later in the book, you'll see that you have to build a targeted social network that gives you the best returns.

Who Is Using MySpace Marketing?

I've been approached by businesses of all flavors for help with increasing their presence on MySpace. Most are already active MySpace users but don't really understand how it can be used for marketing. Typically they expect massive and immediate returns. When this doesn't happen, they might get frustrated and move on to other means of advertising. It also seems that for many, MySpace marketing is their first experience with marketing in general. The result can sometimes be a disorganized and ineffective campaign. If this is the case with you, don't worry. This book will give you great advice that you can apply to just about any kind of online marketing you undertake. Let's take a look at few companies using MySpace marketing to learn from their experience.

Online Retail Websites

Michael Holmes, owner of r3mnant.com, sells rock-and-roll-inspired clothing through an online retail store. He admits he owes a lot of his success to his marketing efforts on MySpace. During the planning stages for his business, he quickly identified MySpace as a critical platform for promotion because it included such a large amount of his demographic (high school students). It was clear that if his brand were to succeed, it had to be embraced and even endorsed by the MySpace community. Additionally, with MySpace, not only can Michael see his customers, but he also can delve deeper into their personalities and preferences. Figuring out what makes them tick (and, in this case, click) allows r3mnant.com to stay ahead of fashion trends in an industry that is notorious for "in today, out tomorrow."

Through MySpace Holmes was able to showcase the company's products and interact with customers. When you visit the r3mnant.com MySpace profile, you'll find over 800 comments from friends, with most including positive feedback about the clothes. This adds instant credibility to the brand, which is very important to r3mnant.com's (and most other) demographics. When a potential customer sees his friends adding these comments and endorsing the clothes, he might click through to the website and make a purchase as well. The fact that many r3mnant.com customers also enjoy taking pictures of themselves in their new clothes doesn't hurt either. Many of r3mnant.com's customers have taken pictures in their new clothes and uploaded them as profile pictures. Organically, the r3mnant.com brand is now part of the community itself, instead of being viewed as just another advertisement.

Although Holmes certainly took a risk by centering all his marketing efforts on MySpace, his gamble has more than paid off. His MySpace page now enjoys a steady flow of targeted traffic and sales thanks to the more than 19,000 friends who belong to his social network. Like the business itself, the MySpace profile is constantly evolving to include the latest products, news, giveaways, specials, and more. With the recent addition of shareable banners and a street team, Michael has created a viral marketing campaign that extends the brand's reach even further. I asked Michael if he planned to expand into more traditional types of advertising, but he responded, "As far as we are concerned, there is no other medium that could offer us the return that MySpace has."

Figure 1.2 shows r3mnant.com's MySpace page. You can find it at www.myspace.com/revoltrevoltrevolt.

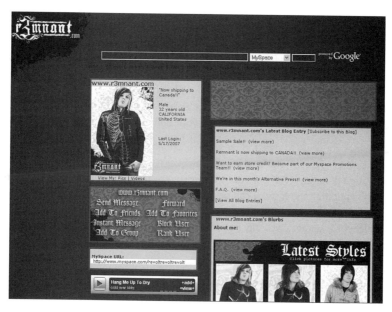

Figure 1.2
An edgy look and feature-rich profile give r3mnant.com the most traction for its MySpace marketing efforts.

Niche Products or Services

If your promotion fills a specific niche, MySpace is a *great* place for your advertisement. With its huge member base and detailed search options, you can locate your demographic with precision never before seen. When users create their MySpace profiles, they include lots of (in some cases, too much) personal information and preferences. Have a promotion you want to market to only 25-year-old women from California? No problem. Have a promotion you want to market to only people in a specific zip code? No problem. Have a product you want to market to only single 25-to-30-year-old male Led Zeppelin fans who went to a specific high school? Believe it or not, that's also not a problem.

When I originally started experimenting with MySpace marketing, it was for my website, customeuroplates.com, where I sell European license plates. This is certainly a niche product, with a primary demographic of 25-year-old males who own a Volkswagen. After trying many other online marketing campaigns, I was not getting the returns for my advertising dollars. On the Internet a niche market can still be a very large one. The difficulty with marketing there is that although people may want your product, they often don't know where to find it. In this case it's sometimes up to you to find them. I quickly discovered that thousands of people on MySpace met my criteria. Eventually I built my profile to 10,000 targeted friends, whom I continue to market to today.

I was able to find these 10,000 friends simply by using the MySpace search features and delivering a compelling message. Because users list things such as interests, location, and other personal information, it's not difficult to find them. In this case, some of the techniques employed included locating related groups on MySpace (we learn about using MySpace groups in Chapter 6, "Precision Targeting Your Demographic") and getting the right message to the right folks. You'll find that once you begin to drill down through your demographic on MySpace, you'll find more and more pockets of your demographic throughout the site.

The results? Sales continue to rise, and we receive valuable customer leads and feedback through our profile each day. The best result, however, is that we have situated our products as part of a huge community of our very specific demographic. In this medium, adding to the community and helping it grow can be more important than just advertising to it. Our MySpace page also allows us to actively participate with our customers on events and sponsorships. A niche market also typically has what you might call a "scene" that encompasses the demographic. It's important that your product is part of this scene, and MySpace makes this very easy.

As you start to build connections in your relevant scene, your promotion also receives the benefit of branding with that scene. Users begin to identify your friends with their friends and hopefully help to contribute in some way. One way we contributed was to track down other organizations, such as car clubs and car shows. MySpace helped to make it easy to connect and collaborate with several organizations full of our demographic. By trading promotional materials with these piers, we were both able to extend our reach even further.

Figure 1.3 shows customeuroplates.com's MySpace page. You can visit us at www.myspace.com/europeanlicenseplates.

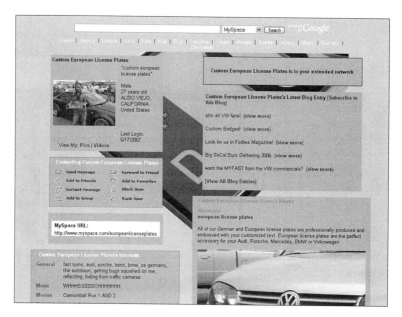

Figure 1.3
An interactive license plate maker allows visitors to demo the product and click through to purchase.

Self-Promoters

Let's say your advertisement or promotion is, well, *you*. Thankfully on MySpace there really doesn't seem to be any concerns for narcissism; in fact self-promotion is probably one of the most common types of marketing you'll find. Musical artists were the first to embrace MySpace as a self-promotion platform. Now an increasing number of other self-promoters are joining in as well. Everyone from realtors to salespeople and many others can use MySpace as a networking tool. This is great for generating new leads and business opportunities or just getting your face and message in front of influences of your industry.

Tila Tequila

One of the best examples of self-promoters is MySpace's most popular user, Tila Tequila (www.myspace.com/tilatequila), shown in Figure 1.4. Before MySpace, Tila was one of the first members of Friendster (www.friendster.com), and she became similarly popular there. In fact, she was a little too popular. Her page was causing a strain on the Friendster servers, so she got deleted. When MySpace cofounder Tom Anderson heard about this, he invited her to MySpace, and she joined as one of the founding members. Tila currently has about 1.8 million friends she markets various products to with MySpace marketing.

Tila's success story is unique. She has been able to launch a full-time career thanks to MySpace. She has appeared on several magazine covers, launched a clothing brand, and even released an album. Although some of her success can be attributed to her early arrival on

MySpace and sex appeal (as you can see in Figure 1.4), there is still plenty of room for others to do the same. This can apply to just about anyone or any type of service you provide. Finding new contacts and clients online has always been a challenge, but your social network can provide a wealth of both.

Figure 1.4

One of the most viewed pages on MySpace belongs to Tila Tequila.

So if you want to get your name out there, or you just think you're great and you want others to know it, MySpace is a smart place to be. Because MySpace pages tend to get high placement in search engines, this is also a great way for people to find you. Just make sure that the message they see is appropriate for your profession and won't damage your image. On more than one occasion people have lost a job or a business deal due to racy pictures on their MySpace profiles. While a picture of you drinking with friends may be a good memory, it's probably not a good thing if you are marketing yourself or a service.

Branding

Multi-national brands like Burger King, Toyota, and many others have flocked to MySpace for branding and new-product releases. These companies tend to have large marketing budgets, so they can afford some of the paid MySpace advertising services, in addition to just creating a page. Movies such as *300* and *Iron Man* have sponsored new MySpace features with great success. However, if your branding needs aren't quite as grand, or you are just starting out, MySpace marketing can also work for you. Smaller independent brands actually do very well because many users prefer them to the larger and more mainstream brands. Small and independent brands of all types fair very well on a service like MySpace. Here the platform is agile and relevant, much like your own independent brand. Here you can routinely deliver new messages through MySpace bulletins, blogs, and more. A major challenge many marketers face when trying to brand a promotion is keeping the message fresh. Keeping a well-maintained and active MySpace presence can greatly help to reduce the fatigue commonly associated with branding anything.

Other Businesses

No matter what your business or promotion is, chances are MySpace marketing is right for you. If you can benefit from additional web traffic, leads, or branding, MySpace can provide all of these. Let's focus on a few businesses and industries that can and have used MySpace marketing.

MySpace marketing is really great for the following:

Age Groups (% of Users)	Retail	Entertainment	Local Businesses	Musicians
12–17 (25%)	Clothing	Actors/Actresses	Restaurants	Bands
18–24 (20%)	Electronics	Filmmakers	Realtors	Solo Artists
25–35 (10%)	Niche Items	Comedians	Trainers	Songwriters
36+ (45%)	Music	Writers	Tattoo Shop	Singers

Websites	Events	Services	Services continued	Services continued
Ecommerce	Night Clubs	Lawyers	Photographers	Artists
Blogs	Concerts	Consultants	Models	Marketers
Communities	Car Shows	Writers	Insurance	Screen Printers
Personal Sites	Live Performances	Notary	Promoters	
eBay Stores				

This is just a sampling of the types of companies and individuals using MySpace marketing today. If you find your promotion listed in the table, then you are already in a great position to benefit from it. If you are not listed, don't worry—through the course of this book, you'll learn valuable tips that can be applied to any promotion. It would be difficult, in fact, to even come close to listing all the other types of businesses using MySpace marketing. MySpace marketing is great for just about anyone with that entrepreneur spirit. Many (if not most) of the marketing found is created by just this type of individual.

How MySpace Marketing Works

You are probably wondering how a business or promotion can fit into a network structure based on friends. You also might be thinking that businesses don't have friends—they have customers or clients. However, things are different now. Companies are trying to turn customers into not just friends, but fans. Businesses that can do this usually receive returns they never expected and waves of new customers. Some examples include Starbucks, Napster, and In-N-Out Burger in California. All three companies found themselves becoming household names after large communities of people rallied around their products.

Today, any size of business can create the same effect by using MySpace marketing to create an online version of a passionate community. This can be beneficial to promotions that already have a large real-world community, but it's even better for new endeavors. I'm sure your product, band, or promotion is great, but without a community behind it, who will talk about it and, most importantly, tell their friends? Word-of-mouth or referral marketing can be the most powerful type of marketing. It's also one of the most inexpensive because it happens organically and in some cases at no expense.

Additionally, a MySpace page offers another piece of real estate on the Internet for your pro-motion. You may already have a website (if you don't, you should) and other material online. However, a social network can greatly increase your reach. Also, as you may have discovered, it's difficult to get people to visit your website at first. MySpace can help jump-start your other online endeavors by sending qualified traffic to them right away. In addition to creating web traffic and generating leads, MySpace is a great place for branding. This can apply to products, musicians, and even companies looking to market locally.

Two Things to Consider

Before we get started, let's cover two common issues with MySpace marketing. Keep in mind that some types of businesses are not right for MySpace marketing. MySpace users today also have more spam controls than ever; they can report abusive profiles, which are typically deleted. Obviously, this is something we want to avoid with our MySpace marketing.

Adult Content

Because the website allows members younger than 18 to participate, any type of adult mate-rial is not allowed. Unfortunately, because of the great marketing opportunity MySpace repre-sents, these kinds of sites are littered throughout in the form of fake profiles. These typically take the form of a profile bearing an incredibly attractive girl who is just dying to be friends with you. These profiles also usually contain links to webcam websites or even malicious code to steal your password. It's a rather nasty little cottage industry that is best to avoid. After much concern from parents and schools, MySpace now does a much better job of locating and deleting these profiles. In fact, many of these profiles are removed quickly before causing too much distress.

Spammers

A few marketers have taken MySpace marketing too far and participate in what can only be referred to as "spammy" behavior. They create fake profiles and blast their advertisements to thousands of members. Most of the time, the promotions are for affiliate or questionable multilevel marketing (MLM) programs that few users have interest in. I can't stress enough that this book is not for this type of marketing, and I encourage you to avoid these types of businesses. In addition to polluting the MySpace community, these promotions just make it more difficult for those who are looking to start organic and ethical marketing campaigns. In this book, you'll learn to market successfully and correctly without raising spam flags.

What to Expect from MySpace Marketing

Creating your MySpace presence requires some commitment. You can't just throw up a profile and walk away from it. It takes a great deal of effort to build and maintain your social network. In this book, you will learn some tips and shortcuts, but if you are not passionate about your promotion and community, you probably won't get very far. Try to think of your MySpace page and social network the same way you approach your business. Keeping this in mind, there is always room for improvement and growth. Just like with your business, this sometimes takes time.

Many times clients have approached me and energetically said things like "I want one million friends ASAP." However, you need to keep your goals within a realistic reach. Instead of looking for a quick fix, take the time to secure the longevity of your marketing campaign and impact. This truth is, getting millions of friends is not the only way to launch a successful MySpace marketing campaign. Focusing on a much smaller but highly targeted number of friends for your social network can give you the great result as well.

You also need to be ready for any feedback you receive, whether good or bad. Take the good feedback as things you are doing right, and use any criticism to improve your business and marketing materials. On MySpace, your social network is just that—very social. In the past, this very vocal (and, of course, public) criticism was many companies' worst nightmare. Now it's up to people behind the message to stand out and join the conversation. It's a unique opportunity for any marketer to expand their reach and learn about the next generation of online advertising. Now that you are ready (and hopefully excited), the next chapter shows you how to start booming your business with social networks.

Preparing Your Business for MySpace

A MySpace marketing campaign should be approached like any other advertising efforts you undertake. This requires a certain level of preparation to execute successfully, something many skip when they jump into this new medium. Without a solid plan and good grasp of the community, your promotion will most likely fall flat with this crowd. In this chapter we are going to take your through how to prepare your business for MySpace.

We start with what materials are needed to get started. We take a look at all the individual pieces needed from the artwork, to dynamic elements like videos and even people. In concert, these elements will be used across all of your MySpace marketing campaigns. Finally, and perhaps most importantly, let's review and set some expectations for your promotion. It's difficult not the get a sense of eagerness when approaching MySpace marketing, after all most of this work is actually fun. That in mind, it's also important to understand the eco system and user behaviors before jumping right in.

An important take away for MySpace Marketing is simple, your promotion should not read like an advertisement; instead, it should be an extension of your business or brand. In the world of MySpace, a promotion can be much more than a run-of-the-mill advertisement. The dynamic platform that is MySpace allows for interactivity from your target market like never before. This power of the crowd can be a great tool for your business if leveraged correctly. Be ready to keep an open mind and be forward thinking while we take a look at a few items to prepare before getting starting.

Be Ready for Feedback (Good and Bad)

The same thing that has initially kept shy marketers from entering the space has turned out to be the most powerful. Be prepared for viewers of your promotion to display their likes and dislikes for the world to see through comments and blogs on MySpace. On MySpace, it's important to accept the bad feedback with the good you receive—trust me, you'll get plenty of both. Positive feedback adds credibility, but negative feedback is just as valuable, if not more so. Take any negative feedback and objectively follow what others have to say; use the knowledge gained here to retool where needed. Reply to each negative comment with a positive spin and solid acknowledgment.

You'll find that people aren't afraid to say what they feel when posting online, and this is especially true on MySpace. This very vocal user base is going to sing your praises or completely trash your promotion. In a worst-case scenario, you still have the ultimate power to remove a negative comment as long as it's part of your MySpace page and not someone else's. If the conversation is occurring on other members profiles this is a great chance to join and respond. Always keep a calm head and kill them with kindness as they say. The last thing you want is to get into an online fight in any public area of MySpace.

Online feedback is now part of a new and more open marketing movement. It can best be summed up as "running naked." Companies are exposing themselves online through social networks, blogs, and online videos because they understand that this is what the consumer wants. The Internet Generation has a huge appetite for content online, and companies are struggling to meet this need. They want a closer look at who you are and how your business works. Exposure has long been taboo in the world of business and marketing because it can also imply risk. Today, whether your business is large or small, the consumer wants a more intimate look at who you are and what you have to offer. By harnessing the power of a social network, you help satisfy their curiously while at the same time getting your message across. Now more than ever it's up to you listen back.

Get or Create Your Marketing Artwork

Presentation is very important on MySpace, so you'll want to gather and create the proper artwork to get your message across. A MySpace page can be customized to include just about anything, including images, text, videos, and even your own color schemes. If you have a designer, work with him or her to create and format the artwork you plan to use on your MySpace page.

Clicking on any of the featured profiles from the homepage should give you some great ideas to get you started, but the more unique your look and feel, the better. In fact I recommend dedicating some serious time to first observing how others use creative artwork on MySpace. You can easily find many examples under the vertical based profiles like music, comedians, and film. Here you'll find most profiles feature custom images throughout with each having a unique call to action for the user. Once you've seen a few good examples, think about how you can apply what they've done to your own promotion.

There are a few stand bys when it comes to MySpace marketing artwork. These include things like logos, wallpaper, advertising banners, and product images, which are discussed in the next sections. These few simple elements should be made collected before getting started with MySpace marketing. You'll have many opportunities to incorporate them into your campaign so its best if they are close at hand. Now let's take a closer look at each of these items.

Logos

First let's talk about using logos for your promotion. Logos can be a great way to add some additional branding to any MySpace page. You'll want to use them sparingly however, as too many logos may make a profile appear overly commercial. You may want to also include logos for other brands you have a partnership with. This helps to build some credibility to users who might recognize your promotions partners.

For the actual logo image file you'll want to use a file that is no larger than 200KB. Since many logos come in much larger files and various other file types, make sure you also have a "web-ready" version of your logos. If a designer created your logo, you can simply ask for few down sized version of your image at 72 DPI and in JPG format. Your logo should be clean and simple, as seen in Figures 2.1 and 2.2.

Figure 2.1
Example of a logo with a white background.

Figure 2.2
Example of a logo with a dark background.

Wallpapers (aka Backgrounds)

Just like your desktop wallpaper, your MySpace page can also have custom wallpaper. On MySpace, wallpapers will appear behind the actual profile itself. This is a quick way to add a lot of impact to your profile, but don't overdo it. MySpace pages are notorious for having over-the-top backgrounds and colors that distract from the page's content. In some cases, this can even make the page hard to read, which is the last thing you want. A simple and effective wallpaper is best, as seen in Figure 2.3.

As you can see, the middle of the wallpaper is kept open and is usually one solid color. The middle is where the main content of the MySpace page goes, so you'll want to make sure it's easy to see. The image should be 1024×768 pixels in size, leaving 800 pixels open in the middle. This leaves the sidebars to showcase anything from your logo to other imagery. Today many users have screen resolutions, even larger than 1024×768 pixels. To solve this problem you can create even larger backgrounds in sizes like 1280×1024 and even larger. Additional you can still effectively display smaller wallpapers by centering your image and using a background color that matches your wallpaper. We learn how to do this in Chapter 4, "Designing Your MySpace Profile".

Additionally, these wallpapers you create can be used by other members who help your brand reach new friends outside of your social network. If you can create a few of these, offer them to visitors on your MySpace page. Here is a great way to help spread your promotion and offer a freebie to your profile visitors. You'll find most MySpace users have added a custom wallpaper to their profile. This allows them to express themselves and stand out from the millions of other profiles on the site. If you plan to offer free wallpapers, try to create fun and creative images others will want to share. It's perfectly fine to feature your promotion or just a simple logo within these free wallpapers you give away.

Bands for example can really take advantage of this by getting fans to use wallpapers that feature the group or artist.

Figure 2.3
Wallpaper sample, which displays the company's logo and color scheme.

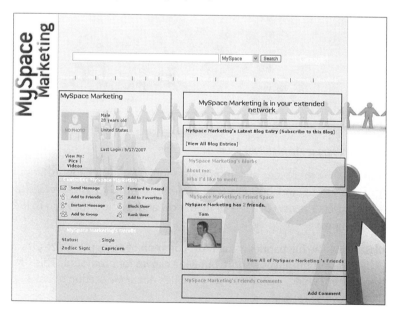

Figure 2.4
MySpace page with custom wallpaper installed.

Advertising Banners

Advertising banners are used throughout the web to drive traffic and much more. On MySpace you can also deploy some of the same techniques used by websites that display banner ads. Let's say you want to direct a visitor to an external websites, such as your official site or an ecommerce website. By mixing in banner ads within your usual MySpace content, you can quickly create an avenue for building traffic to your website.

You may have already created some online adverting materials, such as banner ads or digital flyers. Gather any relevant artwork like this for inclusion in your MySpace page. These images should be no larger than 400 pixels so they fit properly into the MySpace page. I've found that 400×400 pixel boxes work great, as seen in Figure 2.5.

Figure 2.5
Use existing advertising art to highlight your call to action.

There are also many other types of common sizes for advertising banners. Since web surfers quickly adjust to (and ignore) advertisements, its good to use several sizes to keep things fresh. Let's review of a few of them now and see how they can fit into your MySpace marketing.

- **Full Banner:** The full banner is the most common of advertising sizes. It's size of 468 by 60 pixels produces a short, but wide canvas for promotion. This size of advertisement works well within your profile's *About Me* section or any MySpace bulletin.

- **Square Button:** The square button is just that, a square (normally 125 x 125 pixels) that looks like a small button. These can fit just about anywhere including your profile's interests section and even as photo captions.

- **Skyscraper:** A skyscraper is a skinny and tall advertisement normally 160 by 600 pixels. These are some of the larger types of ads and give you a lot of room to convey your message. While not always a perfect match for MySpace, they can used in blog posts and bulletins.

- **Half-Page:** The half-page advertisement is one of the largest ones you'll find out there. It takes up 300 by 600 pixels, roughly half of many computer screens out there. On MySpace this type of ads works best at the top of bulletin or blog posts. It can also be placed at the very top of the MySpace profile for a nice (all be it loud) promotion.

Product Images

If you are selling a tangible item, you'll want to showcase this on your MySpace page. Make sure you have some good images of your products; you'll be able to incorporate these in several places on your MySpace page. When you have new products, MySpace is also a great place to advertise them, as seen in Figure 2.6.

Figure 2.6
Michael with r3mnant.com showcases new products and encourages visitors to click through to the website to learn more.

If you don't have any artwork or access to a graphic designer, don't worry—there is also help for you here as well. A wealth of websites offer free MySpace layouts and graphics. This is an easy way to add a high impact and professional look to your MySpace page. Later, I'll show you some of the best of these sites and help you incorporate their graphics into your profile.

For the "do it yourself" crowd interested in creating their own artwork, check out Gimp (www.gimp.org). They offer free graphic design software with features comparable to what you would find in Adobe Photoshop. Just be careful with any artwork you create and try to keep the level of quality very high. It's very easy to see who the amateurs are when it comes to creative materials, and bad creativity can affect the entire marketing campaign. When in doubt, contact a graphic designer for help; the cost will be more than worth it, and your campaign will have the polished look it needs.

Widgets

A very effective use of artwork includes elements users can interact with or, better yet, take with them. Commonly referred to as "widgets," these are usually small Flash applications that include games or other features. MySpace will allow most types of widgets as long as they meet their quality standards. This means the widgets must not pose a security risk to MySpace users or be deceptive in any way. Since widgets are hosted on web server outside of MySpace, they do present some risks for the service. However if your widget plays nice with the service, it's a great way to feed updated content directory to your profile and future promote yourself.

For those of us who are programming challenged, SpringWidgets (www.springwidgets.com) lets you create your own custom widget—no experience required! This can even be something as simple as a banner or wallpaper image the user can take and display on his or her profile. However, it can be expanded to include many other things, such as a mini version of your online store, as seen in Figure 2.6, or an RSS feed from your existing blog. The MySpace crowd loves these features and can help greatly by redisplaying your promotion in various formats on their MySpace page.

Small mini games are also very popular widgets on MySpace and other social networks. You'll see advertisements based around these mini games throughout the sites from paying advertisers. These are usually very quick and basic games to engage the viewer and get them to play. Upon beating the game, the viewer is then directed to the advertiser's website. You can create your own mini game with websites like Pic To Game (www.pictogame.com), which offers several options. These can be shared in several places on your MySpace page, including your blog, comments, and bulletins.

If you plan to deploy any type of widget make sure you are also encouraging users to share them as well. You can do this by offering what is called the embed code to anyone viewing them. This is the same code you use to add these elements into your profile. By offering a link to somewhere a user can copy this embedded code, you can increase the items audience. Each time another member embeds it into their profile, or a user comment, that's one more piece of real estate you can use for promotion.

Figure 2.7
This Zappos.com widget can be shared and posted on any MySpace page. Let others do the marketing for you!

Creating Videos

YouTube changed the way we view video online, and in the process, empowered millions to broadcast themselves. Creating a "viral video" today now represents a huge opportunity for gathering web traffic and eyeballs, so naturally many have tried to capitalize on this. Some of the most popular videos on YouTube have been viewed over 20 million times—that's more than many prime-time TV shows.

Not wanting to be left behind, MySpace has also added a feature that enables users to upload videos and share them with the MySpace population. With MySpace's huge user base, they have quickly become the number-two online video destination on the Internet. Although you should upload promotional videos to both services, MySpace's video service also enables you to easily integrate videos into your MySpace page.

Creating that killer video is easier said than done, but if you succeed, your promotion can reach new heights online. One great example of this is a series of videos from Blendtec, a company that manufactures high-end kitchen blenders. With their "Will it Blend?" videos, a company representative blends everything from iPods to light bulbs in an over-the-top demonstration of their product's power. For their creative idea, the company's videos have been viewed by millions of people and generated traffic to their website (www.willitblend.com). The notoriety has increased sales and even landed the company on shows like *The Tonight Show* with Jay Leno.

Figure 2.8
The "Will it Blend" video series has been a very effective and fun marketing video for Blendtec.

Although I can't tell you what the next great idea is for a viral video, I can offer some help. If you're a company, show some of the behind-the-scenes workings of your company in a humorous manner; if you are an artist, showcase a recent performance or event. By doing this, you'll be able to offer your viewers a deeper connection to your promotion. Leverage traffic from the video by including a link to your web site or MySpace page at the beginning of the video, similar to credits for a movie. Last, think out of the box on this one; think of commercials that catch your attention because they are funny, shocking, or just something your demographic can really relate to. Take an idea and run with it, and watch user's responses to the videos closely. We learn additional video techniques in Chapter 8, "Using Video With MySpace".

Find a Mascot

A mascot can be the staple of any good promotional campaign. From the very first mascot the Michelin Man, to today's Jared from Subway, mascots have long served as a great promotion vehicle for marketers. On MySpace, it is not different; in fact using a mascot for your promotion can greatly improve your results. Because the website is based so heavily on its social aspects, you might find by adding a face to your MySpace page instead of just a logo, users will be more inclined to make a connection and join your social network.

The Infamous Tom

Figure 2.9
The iconic image of Tom Anderson that welcomes all new MySpace members.

You'll notice that when you first create a MySpace profile, you are automatically friends with someone named Tom. Most users think this is the real profile of Tom Anderson, the President of MySpace, but the reality of this has been up for debate recently. It is now clear that the infamous Tom profile isn't actually used by Tom Anderson himself. In fact, he has another private profile that he uses to communicate with friends and colleagues on MySpace. Tom Anderson was originally hired as a PR agent, so it was a natural choice to use his image as the face of MySpace. His profile helped to add a personal touch to the website and showcased the social features available. Yes, even MySpace itself has used a profile as a platform to market, promote, and interact with others.

In this book, we will reveal how you can utilize some of the same strategies that made MySpace such a huge success. Search your brand and see if you too can use the mascot approach. This is especially great for artists and self promoters because you already have several options for a mascot, including yourself. For larger brands or services, try to translate this into a person or character who represents the company and promotion. Give your marketing a face and some human feel before you join the online conversation.

Existing Contacts and Address Books

Later in the book, I'll show you how you can leverage existing contacts and include them in your MySpace marketing. To do this, you'll want to consolidate your contact lists into one easy-to-manage file or address book. Take any email addresses you've gathered from your website or from business cards you've collected over the years. If you can, import these into a web-based email account such as Gmail or Hotmail. MySpace offers some great invite tools that will not only tell you which contacts are already a MySpace member, but also invite anyone who isn't a member to join the website. These users can be some of the most valuable to have, as they are already familiar with the promotion and hopefully are satisfied enough to join your social network and add positive comments.

Getting Started

Creating a MySpace Profile

nyone can create a MySpace page for free; the process is pretty straightforward. To get started, you just need some basic information and a valid
email account. For some, this might be your first time creating a social network profile. Although there are a few important things to keep in mind, many
options can always be changed at a later time. When creating your profile, it is
not entirely important to have everything in place right out of the gate.

If you do, however, have some of your artwork available, you can begin adding
these images during the signup process. Don't feel you need to load all your
images and content at this time. Later in this book, we will go into further detail
on how to best utilize your MySpace page. For now, a company logo or single
image can get you started on your path to MySpace marketing success. In this
chapter, we are going to look at just a few things to keep in mind during the
signup process. To get the most out of your MySpace marketing, there are a few
important things to consider.

Because MySpace offers several inner communities, you might find your promotion fits better in one of them. Many users don't know about the different profile types—for example, for a band or comedian. If your promotion falls under
one of these communities, your profile gets a few specific bells and whistles
and better placement on the website. We are also going to look at how to select
the best MySpace URL. This gives you a private address like www.myspace.com/
YourName. This is very important to your MySpace marketing because this
address can be used on all your promotional materials. Now it's time to take
those first steps and create your own MySpace profile.

Already Have a MySpace Profile?

Even if you already have a MySpace page, you might want to consider opening a new one for each of your promotions. For active MySpace users, sometimes it's not a bad idea to separate your business from real-life friends. For one thing, some of your existing friends might not appreciate you marketing directly to them. It also saves your promotion from any damage if inappropriate material appears on your personal page. I usually recommend that clients maintain a private profile for themselves. If you want to, invite existing friends to your other pages as well.

Selecting a Profile Type

MySpace has several different profile types, so let's make sure you are getting started with the correct one. MySpace currently offers the options described in the following sections.

Personal Page

http://signup.myspace.com/index.cfm?fuseaction=join

The personal page is the most commonly used profile on MySpace. It's also the default type of profile used when you click Sign Up from the home page. This type includes the standard features such as customization, and it appears in the MySpace people search.

Music Artist Profile

http://signup.myspace.com/index.cfm?fuseaction=bandjoin

Musicians and bands should create a music artist page. This type of profile gives you a few extra features, like a built-in music player and some tools for displaying upcoming shows. Your page will also be listed in the artist directory, which is a very popular location on MySpace. Additionally, users can embed your songs into their profiles, which is great for getting your music out there. You can use the preceding link to get started or click the "Music" link in the top navigation followed by the Artist Signup.

Comedian Profile

http://collect.myspace.com/index.cfm?fuseaction=comedianJoin

MySpace recently launched a comedy section of the website, devoted to stand-up comedians. These pages are similar to the music artist pages, where you can post upcoming gigs and display video clips of recent appearances. Using this type of page will also list you in the comedian search and upcoming gigs calendar. You can use the preceding link to get started or click the Comedy link in the top navigation followed by the Comedian Signup.

Filmmaker Profile

http://signup.myspace.com/index.cfm?fuseaction=filmmakerJoin

The film section of MySpace is a valuable place for aspiring filmmakers to showcase some of their work. With this type of page, you can upload your trailers or full-length movies for the community to watch and rate. There is also a great classified section just for filmmakers to find talent for their next project. Because MySpace limits uploads to 100MB, you might need to split up your longer films into several parts. Another technique is to release "teaser" videos, which contain a link to your website. This can help drive traffic from users interested in seeing more of your work. The filmmaker signup is a bit hidden in the site, so be sure to use the preceding link to create this type of profile.

Most people will use the personal page, but if you happen to belong to one of the other categories, be sure to sign up at the right location. These profiles include a few extra features and receive better placement in their respective industries. You can use the URLs just mentioned to locate the correct signup pages or click their pages from the top navigation bar. On the top right of each page, you'll see the signup link for that category, as shown in Figure 3.1. For a personal page, you simply need to click the signup button from the MySpace home page. MySpace also displays options for these special profiles on the right side of the signup page.

Figure 3.1
The Filmmaker Signup link on the MySpace Film category page.

The Signup Process

The signup process itself is quick and easy. As mentioned, be sure to provide a valid email address you can always access. Other than that, you'll just need some basic information about yourself or your promotion. Clicking the SignUp link the top-right corner will get you started in the process. First you'll be presented with the MySpace signup form, where you start to input your information.

The Signup Form

The MySpace signup form is a simple web-based form that collects data about you. Made up of a few basic fields, this data is used for your profile to get you started. Most of this information can always be changed at a later time, but for now, let's take a look at some of the individual fields.

Email Address

Enter your main email address or an address you will always have access to. The address used here will also receive notifications from MySpace about recent activity, such as new messages. These notifications can be adjusted later after the signup process is complete. Using a valid email address is important because it helps MySpace verify you are the owner of a profile should an issue arise.

Password

Your password, of course, is a very important little piece of information. Try to avoid using simple terms, such as names, for security reasons. MySpace profiles are notorious for being hacked and used for unscrupulous means (spamming). A good combination of numbers and letters is one way to add additional strength to your password. Make sure to never enter your password unless you are 100% certain you are at the official MySpace website. Scammers are well-known for setting up dummy MySpace login pages to steal passwords from unsuspecting users.

First and Last Name

Here you can enter your own name or even the name of your promotion. This is one of those settings that can be adjusted later if necessary, so don't feel locked in here. Keep in mind what you use here will be available through the MySpace search tool.

Country, State, and Postal Code

This location information is also used in conjunction with the MySpace search tool. Users can search out other profiles based on location and distance from them. If your promotion is locally based, you'll want to make sure this data is correct. For promotions that are not locally based, consider entering the closest major city. This will give your profile just a little more reach to the audience in that area.

Date of Birth

These pull-down menus enable you to set your age and determine if this information is public or not. In most cases, the profile owner can simply use their own information here. If, however, your promotion is targeted to specific age ranges, you might want to consider using this here. That way, relevant users can easily find your profile through their searching and browsing.

Gender

For profiles that are marketing a person, you'll of course want to select the proper gender here. Some MySpace marketers have been known to play with this field a bit, depending on their target audience. For example, if your audience is male, it's more likely they will be searching out females on the website.

Preferred Site and Language

Because MySpace runs several international websites, you have to choose the appropriate one from the Preferred Site & Language setting. These international websites are separated from each other, so users see only MySpace pages from this chosen preference. In most cases, this choice will be the U.S. site, which is currently the largest. As shown in Figure 3.2, the first page of the signup page is for you to provide your basic user information, such as name, email address, and password.

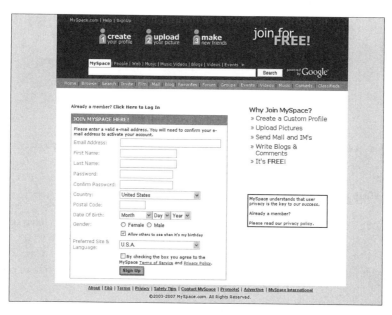

Figure 3.2
The first page of the MySpace signup process.

Verification (CAPTCHA)

To help further prevent automated programs from creating profiles, you are required to pass an image verification. This is called a CAPTCHA. It is used on several places on the website, including comments and the friend request tool. Using this helps MySpace reduce the amount of system abuse by spammers and improve the overall user experience. If you are having trouble reading this image, you can use the Refresh button (the icon with two arrows), as shown in Figure 3.3, to generate a new CAPTCHA image. Don't worry about using uppercase versus lowercase letters; they are not case-sensitive. After entering this code and clicking the terms of service box, click SignUp to go onto the next step.

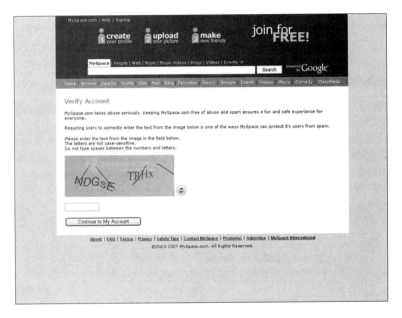

Figure 3.3
This strange-looking image prevents automated robots from creating MySpace pages.

Adding Your First Photo

The next step allows you to start adding photos to your MySpace page. If you have some ready, go ahead and add them by clicking Browse and locating the images on your computer, as shown in Figure 3.4. Clicking Upload sends the file to MySpace, and it is set as your default image. Images should be in JPG or GIF format and no larger than 600KB. Feel free to click Skip this step, because we will cover image management later in the book.

Working with images can be difficult for those who don't have experience with photo-editing software, such as Adobe Photoshop. The price (sometimes more than $500) can also be an issue for some. However, many free alternatives are available online on websites like www.gimp.org. Gimp is very similar to Photoshop, but is offered as free open source software.

After downloading and installing the software, be sure to stop by the tutorials page at http://www.gimp.net/tutorials/. Here you can find some great walkthroughs on Gimp basics and more advanced features. At the very least, this program should help take the frustration out of editing and cropping images. Good presentation of your creative elements is a very important component of MySpace marketing.

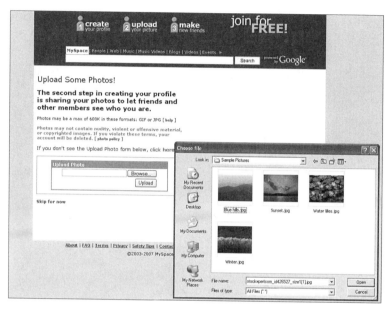

Figure 3.4
Adding the first and default image to your MySpace page.

The MySpace Invite Tool

You're almost there. You should now be at the Invite page, as shown in Figure 3.5. This page allows you to invite your friends to join you on MySpace and become part of your social network. This tool is one of the best but most underutilized marketing tools of MySpace. Since your new MySpace page is not ready for visitors yet, this is another reason to skip this step.

Success!

After this final step, you should see the MySpace Dashboard. You'll notice that you also already have one friend. MySpace cofounder Tom Anderson is every new user's first friend. You can delete him if you like; he won't take it personally. However, most people keep Tom as a friend because this profile is typically used to make announcements in the form of bulletins. The MySpace dashboard displays recent activity on the website from your friend network.

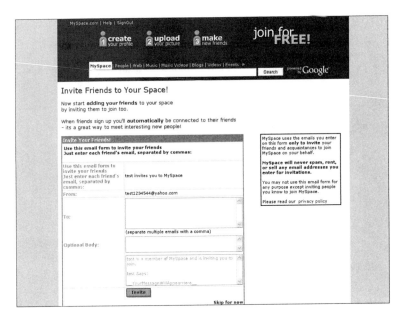

Figure 3.5
The Invite page—a great MySpace marketing tool you'll learn about later.

The MySpace Dashboard

After a successful signup for login, you'll find yourself at the MySpace Dashboard, as shown in Figure 3.6. Everything you need to effectively use the service can be found on this page. It is also used to display the latest activity of your friend network in the "Friend Status" box.

Figure 3.6
The MySpace Dashboard shows you recent activity and gives you access to the many options available for your profile.

Email Verification

Let's take care of two things before moving on to designing your MySpace page. The first is the email verification process. You should see a message in red about this with a clickable link, as shown near the bottom left of Figure 3.7. This sends an email to the address on file that you can use to verify your account. Until this is activated, you have limited access to all the MySpace features. You can't send friend requests or leave comments on other MySpace pages.

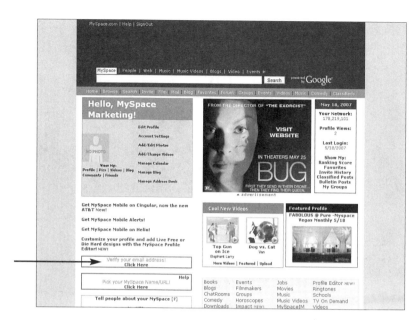

Figure 3.7
Be sure to verify your email address by clicking this link.

Setting Your MySpace Custom URL

The next item is your custom URL setting, which gives you a personal address for your MySpace page, such as www.myspace.com/YourName. This is probably one of the most important settings of your profile because this address can be used for other advertising as well. Your custom URL should be short so that it's easy to remember, but it also should be keyword-rich. The keywords used here will greatly impact your placement in search engines such as Google and Yahoo. MySpace pages rank very high on search results, and this is a great way to drive additional traffic to your MySpace page. To get started click the "create URL" link in the top left of the MySpace Dashboard page.

After starting this process, you'll be required to enter your custom URL twice for verification, as shown in Figure 3.8. You will also receive a few pop-up messages asking you to verify this setting. The reason is that this URL can be set up only once and can never be changed. Really think about what you want to use here because if you change your mind, you'll have to create another MySpace page. If you need to take some time to think about this, you can set up this part later.

Figure 3.8
Setting your custom URL is just like getting a tattoo: it's permanent and a real pain to remove. Make sure you choose the right one for your promotion.

Delving Deeper into The MySpace Dashboard

The MySpace Dashboard, introduced in early 2008, gave a much-needed overhaul to the user interface. Here you have access to just about all sections of the website and your customized options. Some of the features have been grouped into boxes based on their function. If you are new to MySpace, be sure to spend some time poking around the various features. Some of the boxes are interactive and can be customized and even moved around the page. If you click the Home link from any MySpace page, you are also sent here. As you get familiar with this area, let's take a look at a few of the boxes from the middle column. These display real-time MySpace activity and offer a few interesting features.

Friend Status Box

Using the Friend Status box, users can leave a quick message about what they are up to and their current mood. Messages left here get broadcast out to the friend network of the user. Although mostly used for personal casual messages, you can get these updates for your marketing promotions as well. For example, you have news to announce or updates to your MySpace profile or blog. Just look for the Update link in the top-right corner to post your message. It will then be sent out for all to see; if you have something compelling enough, you'll find users clicking through to your profile from here (see Figure 3.9).

Figure 3.9
The MySpace status update tool can also be used for marketing purposes as well.

Friend Subscriptions Box

Friend subscriptions show you more detail about some of the friends in your network. You'll see a real-time update of what they are up to and their activity on the site. Although this is a helpful feature, the real marketing value is getting people to subscribe to your MySpace profile. This may take a little bit of education for some users but offers a much bigger presence for your promotion. Anyone subscribed will see all your activity on the site; when you add a new photo or blog, they will see their activity on their dashboard. Try to incorporate this as a call to action and encourage users to subscribe during your MySpace marketing (see Figure 3.10).

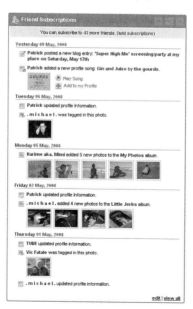

Figure 3.10
Get detailed information about your network with MySpace friend subscriptions.

Friend Space Box

This box is a simple search tool that enables you to select your "Top Friends." MySpace enables each user to select their favorite top 8 to 40 friends and display them with priority on their profile pages. A profile that is featured in someone's top friends list tends to receive more click-through traffic. This traffic also is usually from outside your friend network, presenting the chance to broaden your reach. Similar to the Friend Subscription box, you'll want to encourage your friends to feature your profile in their top listing. Who you feature is up to you. If you have multiple MySpace profiles, this feature can be used to share traffic between them through top friend listings (see Figure 3.11).

Figure 3.11
Quickly find a friend or feature your favorites with the Friend Space box.

Bulletin Space Box

The final box is the Bulletin Space box, which shows the latest bulletins from your MySpace friends (see Figure 3.12). Bulletins are similar to blog posts and are broadcast to everyone in a user's friend network. This feature of the site is probably used most heavily for MySpace marketing and can be one of the most valuable as well. You'll learn more about bulletins in Chapter 10, "Maximizing Bulletins."

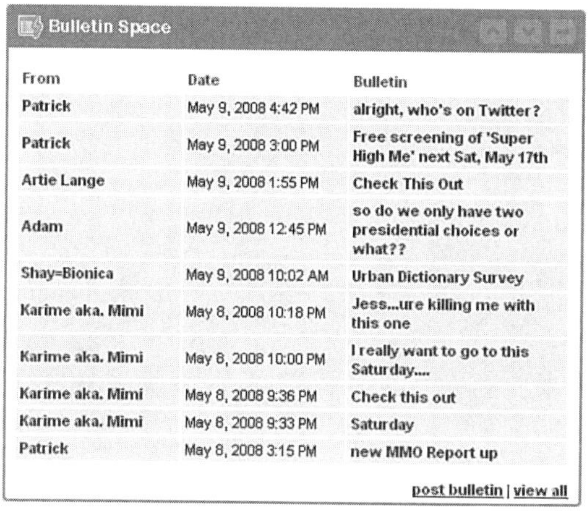

From	Date	Bulletin
Patrick	May 9, 2008 4:42 PM	alright, who's on Twitter?
Patrick	May 9, 2008 3:00 PM	Free screening of 'Super High Me' next Sat, May 17th
Artie Lange	May 9, 2008 1:55 PM	Check This Out
Adam	May 9, 2008 12:45 PM	so do we only have two presidential choices or what??
Shay=Bionica	May 9, 2008 10:02 AM	Urban Dictionary Survey
Karime aka. Mimi	May 8, 2008 10:18 PM	Jess...ure killing me with this one
Karime aka. Mimi	May 8, 2008 10:00 PM	I really want to go to this Saturday....
Karime aka. Mimi	May 8, 2008 9:36 PM	Check this out
Karime aka. Mimi	May 8, 2008 9:33 PM	Saturday
Patrick	May 8, 2008 3:15 PM	new MMO Report up

post bulletin | view all

Figure 3.12
See the latest bulletins from your friends in the Bulletin Space box.

Other MySpace Dashboard Features

Along the left side of the Dashboard, you'll find links to many of the key parts of MySpace. This includes areas of the website such as your personal inbox, profile settings, photos, and more. New users will certainly want to click through here to become familiar with what's available. Even existing users should give this section a scan because there are likely to be some new areas of the website found here. Once you feel comfortable with the lay of the land, it's time to start to further customize your profile and build your friend network.

Designing Your MySpace Profile

N ow that you've created your profile, it is time to delve into designing your MySpace presence. For those with prior experience, you'll be able to pick up some techniques for improving your existing profile. If you have been frustrated in the past or made your profile a complete mess, don't worry. In this chapter, we are going to explore some of the Profile Editor applications available. These tools can really help to make profile design a breeze. We are also going to take a quick primer course on HTML and CSS for more advanced techniques. Finally, we introduce the idea of incorporating dynamic content, like videos, music, and widgets.

Before You Begin

The design of your MySpace page can be one of the most important elements of your MySpace marketing campaign. A messy or amateurish page will not receive the same return as a well-organized and professional one. With millions of MySpace pages out there, it's important for yours to stand out if you want to truly engage a visitor.

In a sense, your MySpace page is just like any other web page, and its design is handled the same way. This means you will be using a combination of layouts, images, and other elements such as Adobe Flash and videos to complete your page. Many users, however, have taken this do-it-yourself nature a little too far, and MySpace now has a reputation for hosting some of the most over-the-top and poorly designed pages on the Internet.

For some, this is their first experience with web design, so you can't blame them too much for overfilling their profile with flashing images and music. Aside from being distracting, too many of these elements can send users running for the Back button in their browsers. Animated images should be kept to a minimum, and any music should require a user action before it begins to play. Keep in mind that visitors to your MySpace page might be at work or school. The last thing they want is a sudden blast of music coming from their computer. Later in this chapter, we cover some of the appropriate ways to handle these types of elements.

Creating a successful MySpace marketing page is a combination of good design and moderation of dynamic elements.

Editing Your MySpace Page

Your MySpace page is broken into several parts, such as the *About Me* and *Who I'd Like to Meet* sections. These are the main sections that appear on the right side of your MySpace page. They are some of the first sections a visitor sees when viewing your profile and are some of the best locations to feature videos and advertisements for your promotion. Users tend to look here closely when browsing through the website, so make sure to get the most of this real estate.

There are also other sections for *Interests*, *Movies*, *Books*, and personal *Heroes* as well. Typically, a user includes some relevant terms for each box. However, you can also use these areas for your marketing needs, too. By placing keywords in the appropriate fields, your demographic can actually find you. After inputting your own terms, these keywords become clickable and lead to other users with the same interests. Think of it as a way for profiles to belong to the same "neighborhood." Placing your promotion in these neighborhoods can really help increase your reach. So try to include terms that your demographic might have an interest in as well.

We also can include web programming languages like HTML and CSS to affect a profile's look and feel. This is done by placing the correct code into one of the available profile boxes. Although this technique is a bit more advanced, even those without prior coding experience can easily get started. In most cases, the code to make these changes is provided for you; all you do is copy and paste it into the correct place.

You can locate the profile management options for your MySpace page after you log in, as shown in Figure 4.1. After clicking Edit Profile, you are presented with many options for providing your information and designing your profile. Customizing your MySpace page is similar to updating a web page, but instead of uploading a file, you create your custom code and paste it into various parts of your page. At some point, this may evolve into a more drag-and-droppable format, but for now, unfortunately it's mostly code-driven.

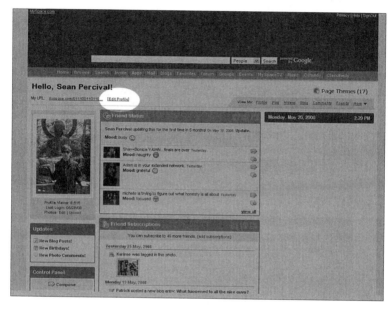

Figure 4.1

The many MySpace page management options, including Edit Profile, which we use for this chapter.

Understanding HTML

HTML, the first programming language widely used on the Internet, stands for Hypertext Markup Language. To this day, it's the primary code used to drive all websites, allowing you to format text, include images, and embed other types of content, such as videos. Because you also use HTML to format and design your MySpace page, an entirely new generation of users has become familiar with it. Although you don't need to be a master of HTML to use MySpace marketing, it is good to know some of its main components.

With some basic knowledge of how these components work, you can begin to refine and expand your usage.

Thousands of little pieces make up the HTML language, but many use the same formatting and options. It's just a matter of tweaking the right part of the code and duplicating existing code to achieve a desired effect. If you've never seen it before, take a look at the code of your favorite websites. It's very easy to do—simply right-click the page (somewhere away from text and images) and select View Source. The larger the website, the more complicated the code will be, so be sure to look at a few simple websites as well.

In the interest of keeping this book focused on marketing, I can't go into all the details of programming for the web. If you are new to using HTML, I recommend picking up a good beginner's guide on the subject. Just make sure you are getting a book appropriate to your level of expertise. Since web programming has many components, some books may cover advanced techniques that can't be used with MySpace. You want the most basic usage possible with examples that are easy to follow and ultimately reproduce.

Recommended Reading

The following books are available from Que and Sams Publishing and can help get you started with HTML. Keep in mind these are not required for MySpace marketing but may prove to be beneficial.

- *Sams Teach Yourself HTML in 10 Minutes, 4th Edition*, Deidre Hayes, 0-672-32878-x
- *Sams Teach Yourself HTML and CSS in 24 Hours*, Dick Oliver and Michael Morrison, 0-672-32841-0.

Finding HTML Help Online

Also tons of resources and tutorials are available online. One website in particular, www.w3schools.com, offers a huge library of hands-on examples and quizzes to test what you've learned. Another way to learn more about HTML is to view the code of an existing website or MySpace page. This really comes in handy when you look at a page and wonder how they did that. However, to make sense of what you are looking at, it is important to understand some of the basics, so let's take a brief tour.

Using Tags

Tags are the most important concept to understand when using HTML because one mistake can affect an entire page. The code works on a simple on and off setting, as shown in the following example of bolding text.

Example

```
Make your text <b> bold </b>. It's easy!
```

How It Looks

Make your text **bold**. It's easy!

In this example, you can see that the tag <b> turns on bold, and </b> turns it off. Failure to turn off this tag (or close it) would cause the remaining text to also appear bold. The closing tag is usually the same code as the opening tag, except with the backslash (/) character preceding it. Tags are always enclosed in angle brackets (<>).

Formatting Text

By default, any text used in HTML is left-justified, with no line breaks between paragraphs. This means that all text runs together, which typically makes it more difficult to read. To create line breaks and new paragraphs, you need to instruct the code to do so.

Example Without Line Breaks

MySpace marketing allows you to better connect with and engage visitors in your MySpace page. Learn how to create a compelling page that gets the viewer excited about your offer. You can use your social network to announce new products and gather feedback from a massive audience. Find out what makes MySpace so cool and learn to leverage its power for your marketing needs. Great for: Bands Small Businesses Events And More!

Example with Line Breaks

MySpace marketing allows you to better connect with and engage visitors to your MySpace page.

Learn how to create a compelling page that gets the viewer excited about your offer. You can use your social network to announce new products and gather feedback from a massive audience.

Find out what makes MySpace so cool and learn to leverage its power for your marketing needs. Great for:

Bands
Small Businesses
Events
And More!

To format this text, I used the following code:

```
<p> MySpace marketing allows you to better connect with and engage visitors to
your MySpace page. </p>
```

```
<p> Learn how to create a compelling page that gets the viewer excited about your
offer. You can use your Social Network to announce new products and gather
feedback from a massive audience. </p>
<p>Find out what makes MySpace so cool, and learn to leverage its power for your
marketing needs. Great for:</P>
Bands <br>
Small Business <br>
Events <br>
And More! <br>
```

The <p>, or paragraph, tag groups a paragraph and creates a large break similar to double spacing. The <BR>, or break, tag creates a single line break and leaves less space between any lines it's used on. You can also produce the same effect as a <P> tag by using two <BR> tags to create a double space. The <BR> tag is also one of the few tags that does not require a closing tag.

Text Alignment

You have a few choices when it comes to aligning your text, such as left, center, and right justification. Although most of the time, you'll use left justification, the others are useful in certain circumstances. Center justification, for example, is great to use for images and headlines.

Example

```
<center>Thanks for Visiting Our MySpace!</center>
```

How It Looks

Thanks for Visiting Our MySpace!

In the preceding code example, we used the <center> tag to justify everything to middle. For other types of justification, you can use the <div> tag.

Example

```
<div align="right">Thanks for Visiting Our MySpace!</div>
```

How It Looks

Thanks for Visiting Our MySpace!

Remember, the <div> tag requires a closing tag. If the closing tag is not included, this justification setting continues throughout the rest of the page. By default, text normally will automatically justify left; in case this doesn't happen, you can use the preceding example while changing the align="right" to align="left".

Creating Links

Including links to other websites can be the most powerful part of your MySpace marketing campaign. Although it's great for a visitor to view your MySpace page, it's even better if you can get that person to your website. On your website, you'll have more control over the content and better access to capture a lead.

Example

```
<a href="http://www.yourwebsite.com" target="_blank">Visit Our Web Site!"</a>
```

How It Looks

Visit Our Web Site!

This example creates a clickable text link that directs the visitor to another website. Whatever you include instead of *yourwebsite* in http://www.*yourwebsite*.com will be the user's destination. We have also added the `target` tag with a property of `_blank`. This tells the browser to open this website in a new window, which is helpful so that the visitor doesn't lose track of your profile while exploring another website.

Using HTML Design Software

Tired of looking at code yet? I wouldn't blame you if you were; this stuff is the, let's say, less-glamorous part of MySpace marketing for many. The truth is, learning HTML code is a book in itself, so we won't focus on it in great detail. If you are interested in learning more, I recommend getting a beginner's book or trying some of the many online tutorials. The real secret of getting started with this is to use some type of HTML editing software. Even the most seasoned HTML coder uses this software to help make this process quicker and easier.

Adobe's Dreamweaver product has been the standard in the web design industry for years and is by far the best. Many of the earlier examples can be done in a simple interface that can be compared to a word processor such as Microsoft Word. Instead of your having to hand-code the text formatting, Dreamweaver lets you apply your styles with line breaks, and it creates the HTML code for you. Dreamweaver also allows you to save copies of your code, which is great for backing up. The software is somewhat expensive ($399), but it's a must for any serious web designer. You can download a free 30-day trial at Adobe's website (www.adobe.com).

The budget-conscious shouldn't be discouraged by Dreamweaver's cost, though, because there are many free alternatives to HTML creation, such as First Page from Evrsoft (www.evrsoft.com) and Kompozer (www.kompozer.net). These programs might not have all the features of the commercial versions like Dreamweaver, but they still can make your life much easier. In addition, you'll learn about some web-based HTML editors later in this chapter.

Using CSS

Cascading Style Sheets (CSS) was created as an extension to HTML; it offers many more formatting options. Due to the setup of MySpace, many of the fun design tricks or hacks are done with CSS. These tricks can include hiding boxes, changing the page layout, and adding rollover effects to text and images, among other things. CSS can be a challenging language to use. Thankfully, most HTML editors also can create this code. The main use of CSS is applying a style to a specific tag, such as the <P>, or paragraph, tag.

Example

```
<style>
p {
 font-family: Verdana;
 font-weight: bold;
 font-size: 14pt;
 font-style: italic;
}
</style>
```

How It Looks

Hello World!

This code says that each time a paragraph tag is used, the text font should be Verdana bold italic in a font size of 14. This style is then applied to all paragraphs on your MySpace page. To learn about the many other uses of CSS, visit www.w3schools.com/css/, where you can follow online tutorials and see examples.

Working with Images

Including images in your profile is a great way to highlight an item and engage the visitor. The first thing to understand with embedding images in your MySpace page is that the images have be hosted somewhere on the Internet first. There are lots of ways to do this. For example, if you have your own website, you can upload these files into your images folder and begin using them. If you can't do this, Photobucket (www.photobucket.com) offers some of the best free image hosting available. When you upload images to Photobucket, the company even helps you generate the HTML code for use with your MySpace page. The Photobucket service is easy to use. MySpace purchased it in 2007 and will likely integrate Photobucket's features into its own website. The following code shows you how to manually embed an existing image into your MySpace page, and Figure 4.2 shows the result.

Example

```
<img src="http://www.yourwebsite.com/images/filename.jpg">
```

How It Looks

Figure 4.2
The cover for this book is on my MySpace page from the Photobucket service.

Making an Image Clickable

You can drive traffic to another website by making the image a clickable link. This is a great place for your call to action, which is where you ask the viewer to take an action such as filling out a form or purchasing something. The following code and Figure 4.3 show the result.

Example

```
<a href="http://www.yourwebsite.com" target="_blank">
<img src="http://www.yourwebsite.com/images/filename.jpg" border="0">
</a>
```

How It Looks

Using this code is similar to creating a text link; however, we have added the `border="0"` property. This helps disable the default blue border that appears on linked images.

Figure 4.3
By clicking this image, page visitors are directed to a new site for more information.

Using Profile Editors

Trying to create all this code can be difficult. For newcomers, I recommend not getting too hung up on learning the language. The secret of MySpace page design is using online profile editors. Many third-party profile editors are available online, including Mashcodes (www.mashcodes.com) and Thomas' MySpace Editor (www.strikefire. com/myspace), but MySpace has started to integrate its own profile editor into the website. This removes many of the headaches of dealing with the design process because you simply select your options, and the service generates the HTML and CSS code for you. The MySpace Profile Editor, shown in Figure 4.4, is located in the top right of your screen after clicking the "Edit Profile" link from your homepage. You can also find it at http://profileedit.myspace.com/index.cfm?fuseaction=profile.editor.

Using the MySpace Profile Editor

The MySpace Profile Editor couldn't be easier to use. This is recommended for those who don't want to have to track down the proper HTML and CSS codes. The interface itself is very intuitive; each option is easy to find and adjusts to your liking. After you have loaded the home page of the editor, you'll have two more tabbed options in the upper-right corner.

Figure 4.4

The MySpace Profile Editor, introduced in May 2007 helps to make the editing process much easier.

The first is Themes; there are several pre-made MySpace themes you can use with your profile. Designs featured here tend to be of high quality and are certainly the easiest way to give your profile some design appeal. To install any of these elements into your profile, simply click the image and hit Save in the Profile Editor to lock in the change. Right after clicking, you'll get a nice preview of how it's going to look.

Figure 4.5

Pre-made MySpace profile designs available in the Themes section of the Profile Editor.

You can locate the heart of the service by clicking the Customize tab in the top right corner. Here you can control just about every property of your MySpace page, including
background, text, images, and links. The MySpace developers were even nice enough to
include an Undo button in case you make a few mistakes before getting it right. A real-
time preview of your MySpace page shows you the results of your changes. Let's take a
look and discuss a few of the Editor's major sections.

Background

The Background tab lets you control the background color and use a background image.
Typically, color isn't that important because most designs use a custom background
image that covers the entire background. As shown in Figure 4.6, you have several
options for displaying your background image.

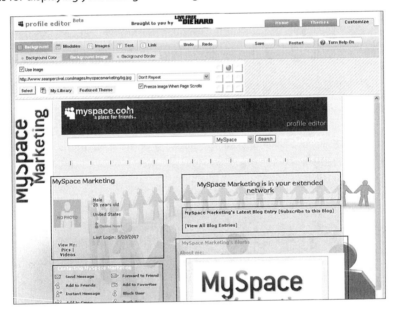

Figure 4.6
Setting up your background image.

The ideal setup is to use an image that is 1024 by 768 in size. Use your favorite photo editor to verify your image isn't too large or too small. Once you have your image ready, you
also need to upload the file to the Internet somewhere. You can then enter the location
of the image in the first box and set the other options to Don't Repeat and Freeze Image.
Unless your background image is a pattern, you'll want to use these settings so that your
custom background remains in place even when the user scrolls the page. If you don't
have a background image, don't worry. Later in the chapter, I'll show you where to find
free ones.

Here is a quick step-by-step guide to add a background image:

1. Under Customize tab, click Background option.

2. Check the Use Image Box.

3. Enter location of image (or select from your uploading MySpace images).

4. Check Freeze Image When Page Scrolls if needed.

5. Select your background repeat options, in most cases you want to set this to "Don't Repeat."

6. Click Save to lock the change.

Modules

The Modules tab contains a wealth of settings for the individual pieces of your MySpace page, such as the contact table, navigation bar, and friend listing sections. You can customize how each box looks, but try not to go overboard. Keeping your design consistent and easy to read goes a long way toward making the most of your marketing. One piece you'll want to pay close attention to is the contact table. This box sits beneath your default page image and includes the links for interaction, including Send Message and Add to Friends, as shown in Figure 4.7.

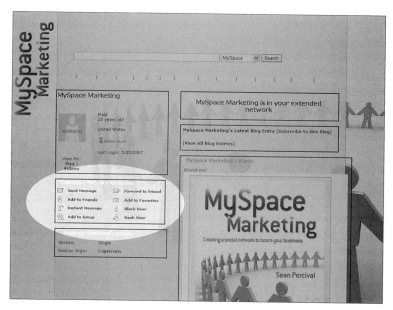

Figure 4.7
The contact table on a MySpace page.

Because getting people to message or add you as a friend is an important part of MySpace marketing, you should make the Add to Friends link stand out. One way to do this is to replace the default look with a custom contact table. This is a single image 300 pixels wide by 150 pixels tall that includes the text for each contact option. It may take a bit of effort to get the alignment right for this image, but as shown in Figure 4.8, the outcome is appealing. You can really get creative with this small piece of real estate and encourage your visitors to make contact.

Figure 4.8
A MySpace page using a custom contact table for further product branding.

Images, Text, and the Link Tab

The remaining tabs of the MySpace Profile Editor are for controlling the presentation of images, text, and any links. I won't go into great detail on all the settings, but keep your overall design in mind when making any changes here. Make sure that text and links are always readable; the best way to achieve this is to use contrasts. If you use a dark background, use light text, and for light backgrounds, keep the text dark or black. Although some of the effects offered here might seem interesting, they can easily distract from your overall marketing campaign.

Finding Free Graphics and Layouts

When people found out they could customize their pages with images and layouts, this spawned a small industry of websites offering free content. Typing MySpace Graphics into Google yields 25 million results of websites full of images and predesigned layouts. Some of the best ones include these:

www.mashcodes.com

www.pimp-my-profile.com

www.bigoo.ws

www.myspacejunks.com

www.xoospace.com

This book's companion website (http://myspacemarketing.ning.com) also includes a large collection of free content. Here you can find many images geared more toward MySpace marketing needs. Because many of these free image sites are for personal users, some of the graphics aren't well-suited for your promotion. Once again we want to use moderation in our profile design and avoid using too many animated images. Pages with these take much longer to load and can annoy many viewers.

Adding Music

Including music in your profile can be a great way to create mood. It's especially benefi-cial for musicians promoting themselves on MySpace. Depending on the type of profile you are promoting, there are several different ways music can be incorporated. As with the design of your MySpace profile, this is also something you want to use with modera-tion. In all cases, I recommend disabling any auto-play features for music. You never know if a visitor will be accessing your page from work or a library. The last thing you want to do is startle them with blasting music and send them frantically looking for the Back button in their browser.

Adding Music to Personal Profiles

Because MySpace already hosts millions of songs, you can easily find available music directly on the website. To get started, click the Music link in the top navigation. In the music area, you'll first see many of the current featured MySpace artists. For promotion here, both big and small artists give you free access to some of their latest hits. To find that specific track, you can try the artist search box located in the upper-right corner of the page.

After you've found your artist, click through to visit his or her MySpace page. Here you'll find a custom music player, as shown in Figure 4.8a. Next to each track name, you'll see a small link that says Add. Click this to add the selected song to your MySpace profile. After doing so, view your profile to verify it's setup correctly and to check if auto-play is enabled. If it is, you'll want to be sure to disable it. To do so, click Edit Profile from your

MySpace dashboard and then click the final tab, labeled Song & Video. In addition to being able to disable auto-play, you can customize your media player as well.

Keep in mind what your MySpace promotion is going to be used for and if using music is appropriate. For example, if there are artists out there that align with your demographic, this is a good time to use it. If your product is more serious or personal in nature, you want to avoid including music.

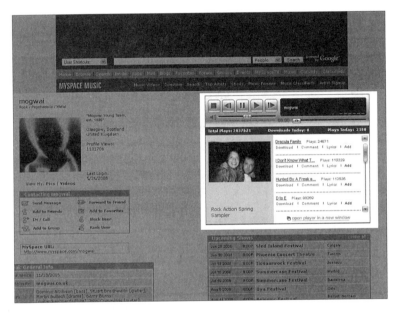

Figure 4.8a
The MySpace music player as seen on the Mogwai Artist page.

Adding Music to Musician Profiles

If you're a musician who wants to upload your own music to MySpace, you'll first want to get your audio files ready in MP3 format. Music pages have a few more options for adding music, such as an upgraded music player and the ability to upload six songs (see Figure 4.9). To manage your songs, click Edit Profile on your MySpace home page and then click the Manage Songs tab. You set your music player settings and manage your songs on the right side.

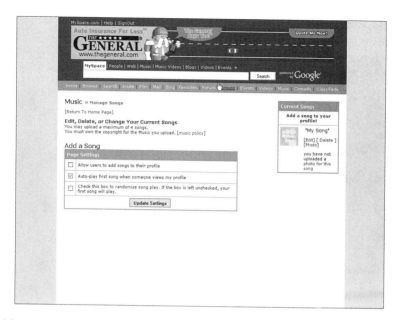

Figure 4.9
The Manage Songs page is a great way to broadcast your latest tracks.

Using Music Player Widgets

There are also several great music player widgets available online as well. Widgets are small pieces of code you add to a web page that are usually small interactive boxes. This code can be added to the *About Me* section of your MySpace page to play your selected tracks. Visit the MP3 section of Widgetbox at http://www.widgetbox.com/tag/mp3 for a nice selection of players you can include in your profile. One other nice thing about widgets is they can be shared with your friends. They can even copy and add your widgets to their profiles as well.

Adding Video

Video is quickly becoming a hot form of viral marketing on the Internet, thanks to websites like MySpace and YouTube. In Chapter 2, "Preparing Your Business for MySpace," we talked about creating a video for your promotion and the value this can offer. If you have video ready, it's now easier than ever to include it on your MySpace page. The first step is to upload your video to MySpace, which you can do from the MySpaceTV section of the website. As shown in Figure 4.10, the MySpaceTV page is a place for both professionals and amateurs to showcase their latest features. Many companies choose to offer exclusives through MySpaceTV in an effort to reach a massive audience.

Figure 4.10
Only a few months after launch, MySpace Video quickly became the number-two online video destination.

Clicking this page's Upload link in the top right corner can get you started with adding video. MySpaceTV accepts just about any format of video up to 100MB in size. After you upload your video, it takes some time to process. After it's done, you can view the video and click the Add to My Profile link to include the clip on your MySpace page. Note that if you upload any adult or copyrighted material, your account will be deleted.

Here is a quick step-by-step guide to adding video:

1. Click Videos from the top navigation menu.

2. Click Upload Videos in the top-right corner.

3. Enter your video information and click Continue.

4. Select the video file from your local computer and click Upload.

5. After upload, view your newly uploaded video.

6. Under the video, click the Add to Profile link to include the video in your profile.

The Future of MySpace Page Design

MySpace is one of the few social networks that allows you to use custom code, as you have learned in this chapter. We have just scratched the surface of some of the options available to you when designing your profile. Many users have gone to great lengths to build code that creates complex page layouts and presentations. Although some services and software are available to ease the design process, it's still very code-heavy, which I know can be an issue for some.

Currently there is a big push in the web development industry to bypass the code and provide users with easy-to-use design tools. As social networks become more main-stream, there is a focus on allowing anyone to create web content without any prior experience. With the recent release of the MySpace Profile Editor, we can begin to see how this can be handled in the future. This is great news if you don't want to get caught up in the language and instead want to spend more effort on the design process. As these tools continue to improve, we are likely to see much of the coding disappear and be replaced with simple web-based tools. Ultimately, designing a MySpace page will resemble using a word processor such as Microsoft Word. You'll be able to drag and drop your content and format your text, colors, and layout with a few clicks of the mouse.

Your approach and page design will also be unique to your offering and develop over time as you become more familiar with the code options (and limitations). Take time to develop your page, but don't be afraid to start marketing it right out of the gate. As you improve your page design, your social network will take notice and will enjoy checking in to see what you've added. In an environment as dynamic as MySpace, a page that continues to evolve will see more return visitors and will capture new ones. The next chapter takes a closer look at the users of MySpace and how they fit into the marketing side of things.

Building Your Friend Network to Maximize Reach

Must-Have Friends

By now you may have noticed that some MySpace users have huge social networks, sometimes with more than a million friends. These members are usually some of MySpace's early adopters who have experienced this popularity over time and through a solid marketing plan. These popular MySpace pages can be beneficial to your promotion if used properly.

I've found that in any type of online marketing, it can be incredibly powerful to research what others are doing, tweak to your needs, and then improve upon. MySpace marketing is no different, so this chapter takes a look at how some of the most popular profiles market themselves. You can learn from their experience, and in many cases, save a great deal of time. Advertising in new media like MySpace can be trial and error. By looking at others, you can quickly learn a few things right, and even a few things wrong.

Tom

www.myspace.com/tom

By default, MySpace president Tom Anderson is everyone's friend. Naturally, he has the largest network. At the time this chapter was written, his network included more than 180 million friends. Tom is typically the first person a new user sees, so this has given him somewhat of a celebrity status. The photo of Tom in front of a whiteboard has become an iconic image for the Internet generation (see Figure 5.1). It has been used on T-shirts and in several Internet parodies.

Figure 5.1
The public profile of Tom Anderson, MySpace president and cofounder.

Tom's placement on MySpace is also interesting from a marketing standpoint. It was a noble experiment in public relations and user experience to make a company's founder so visible and accessible to its users. Initially this made MySpace feel less like a website and more like a cool independent project. This excited millions, and they quickly signed up not only to watch its progress but to become part of it. Tom's profile is a hub for the latest MySpace news using bulletins and blogs to get the word out. What better way to reach your community than to use the tools that drive the community?

Delving a little deeper into the Tom page, you can see how it's also used to market MySpace-related products. Figure 5.2 shows a promotion for Sherwood, a new artist from the MySpace record label (yes, MySpace has a record label). I'll show you how you can deploy some of the same techniques in Chapter 9, "Generating Buzz with MySpace Blogs." This is a very powerful medium on MySpace because many users turn to this section to get the latest updates. The Tom profile is also used to post system news such as technical issues and new features.

As far as where your marketing and Tom's page fit in, there really isn't much to do here. You can keep Tom as part of your social network, but don't do any direct marketing through his page. His profile probably is maintained by staff (he actually uses a separate private profile for friends) and not Tom directly, so marketing done through his page might be considered spam and be deleted. Worse yet, they may remove your profile. As with all aspects of MySpace marketing, moderation is the key. Your promotion should be just enough to get the attention of your demographic without annoying the masses.

Figure 5.2
A sample of a blog promotion from the Tom MySpace page.

Tila Tequila

www.myspace.com/tilatequila

After Tom, the most popular person on MySpace is Tila Tiquila, a model turned Internet celebrity thanks to MySpace (see Figure 5.3). Tila began experimenting with social networks in the form of Friendster.com, where she experienced similar attention and popularity. However, she received a little too much attention, and Friendster was forced to remove her profile. Tom and the other founders were well under way creating MySpace, and they asked Tila to be one of the founding members. Millions of page views later, *Time* magazine included her in its "Person of the Year" issue and called her "The Madonna of MySpace." Her social network is now just shy of 2 million friends, and her page has received more than 67 million visitors.

She has used this exposure to help launch her music career and several Tila Tequila-related products. I tried to contact Tila several times to ask her about how she uses MySpace marketing, but I did not get a response. She is probably too busy recording her new album or hosting her next party. We can, however, get a great idea of her MySpace marketing efforts by simply viewing her page.

Figure 5.3
The official profile of Tila Tequila.

Website

One of the best uses of MySpace marketing is directing visitors from your page to your official website. Once you bring someone to your website, you have more opportunities to monetize the visit or generate a lead. Tila Tequila runs a personal website at www. tilashotspot.com, where visitors can access all things Tila. There is also a subscription service, where for $10 per month, a member gets access to exclusive content like photo galleries, videos, and live-chat sessions. The website also includes advertisements for other Tila-related promotions and a message board for fans.

Music

Lately Tila has been focusing on launching a music career. She has used her MySpace page to generate interest in and sales on her iTunes music store (see Figure 5.4). Although her background is in modeling, she has always been a musician as well and has performed in several bands. She debuted her new music video on YouTube and used MySpace comments to announce its availability on iTunes. This was an effective strategy. The video received over one million views, and her single landed in the iTunes top 100 songs list.

Figure 5.4
Tila uses the top of her page (the most valuable real estate) to announce her new single and music video.

Ringtones

The MySpace demographic is crazy about ringtones (a song that plays when your cell phone rings), so you'll see a lot of advertisements for this service. Many people are happy with their default ring, but many MySpace users customize their cell phones with ringtones they find on the Internet. Tila partnered with Boost Mobile to offer some of her music as ringtones.

This type of marketing is most beneficial to musicians, but the idea can be applied to other businesses as well. If you can align your product with something people will use as a ringtone, I highly recommend looking into this further. Services like Phonezoo (www.phonezoo.com) will create a free ring tone for you based on an MP3 file of your choice. You can even try to sell your ringtones through various services. However, if possible you should give away your ringtones because this will give you much greater reach and increased branding.

Online Gambling

Tila Poker (www.tilapoker.com) offers members traditional online gambling themed around images of Tila. I'm not a big fan of online gambling, and I can't recommend using

MySpace for its promotion. Because MySpace has so many young members, most are ineligible to play. Additionally, the industry itself is filled with fraudulent and deceptive practices. It also causes untold numbers of family problems, such as when someone loses his house due to an online gambling addiction. Try to avoid this industry. There are many other ways to generate revenue online.

Fashion

Clothes and fashion in general translate very well to the MySpace crowd, so many have tried to launch brands from their pages. Tila has tried the same but has had some trouble getting started. It seems with everything else she has going on, she just hasn't had time to focus on this. Her profile now states that an entire new line is on the way. If you want to include clothing as part of your promotion, try Zazzle (www.zazzle.com). It offers simple tools for designing and selling your own clothes and other accessories.

ForBiddeN

www.myspace.com/forbidden

Christine Dolce, or ForBiddeN as she is known on MySpace, has a similar success story to Tila. As one of the first MySpace members, she quickly achieved huge popularity and gathered over one million friends. This former cosmetologist has created a modeling career and appeared in such magazines as *Playboy*, *Rolling Stone*, and *FHM*. *Vanity Fair* called Christine "The Queen of MySpace." Like Tila, she promotes several products on her MySpace page, as shown in Figure 5.5.

Website

For only $14.95 per month, you can become part of the "ForBiddeN Army." Here you get access to exclusive content like photos and videos, and you also get discounts on all ForBiddeN products in the store. Again, sending visitors to your website gives you countless opportunities to market to them. However, I don't think I agree with the subscription model. If a visitor wants to know more about you or your promotion, give him or her as much as you can for free.

As it turns out, ForBiddeN's fans didn't agree with the subscription model either. Just a few months after launching the site, it was closed down. Instead, she now offers a free private community for her many friends. Offering something like this is a great marketing idea because it allows you to take your friends with you. On an outside community like this, you have more control over the layout and better access to individuals as well.

Figure 5.5
The sultry and very popular MySpace page of ForBiddeN.

Fashion

Christine has her own fashion line called Destroyed Denim (www.destroyedbrand.com). She seems to have had more success than Tila with this venture. She has posted to her blog that sales are improving, and new products are added regularly.

Dog Tags

Rock n Tags created a special product line of its customizable dog tags that featured ForBiddeN. While the idea sounds a little kooky, dog tags have always been popular with some segment of youth throughout the years. Promotional items like this can work for other promotions as well. Zazzle (www.zazzle.com) offers a huge line of products, from clothes to coffee mugs to mouse pads.

Perfume

For a short time, Christine sold Forbidden, the scent. This product is no longer featured on her profile, so we can only assume it wasn't the next Chanel No. 5. This is a good example for those experimenting with self-branding: don't take the idea too far.

Other Low Rankers

In all of the preceding cases, much of their popularity is because they were some of the first MySpace members. In addition to having a long history with the site, their profile numbers have a lot to do with their success. When you create a MySpace profile, you are assigned a unique, sequential user number. If you created a profile today, your user number would be something like 215,854,626. Users such as Tila and ForBiddeN have a profile number less than 100,000 because they were some of the first pages created.

Some advantages of these low-ranking user numbers include placement on other MySpace pages throughout the site. If you view any of their friends' social networks, you'll notice that the older the profile, the higher it's listed. You can also see this when using the MySpace search box to find someone. By default, older profiles are displayed as part of someone's "Top 8" friends unless the user customizes this area. This gives these profiles great exposure not only on that person's page but also on the thousands of friend pages that person is part of.

If you are creating a new profile, you don't have much control over what user number you are given. If you have an old MySpace profile in place, you may want to consider using it for your marketing efforts. If your existing user number is low enough (between 1 and 500,000), you may have noticed that you get many messages and incoming friend requests. This is because your profile typically is viewed many more times than a profile that was created yesterday. Using a low-ranked profile or becoming friends with other low-ranked profiles can help you kick-start your own social network.

Featured Profiles

On the MySpace home page you'll find the latest featured profiles. As shown in Figure 5.6, they look like traditional banner advertisements. Prices for this type of placement vary, but rumor has it that some companies pay as much as $100,000 for the spot. When you click these, you'll notice that you don't leave the MySpace site. Instead, you are taken to a MySpace page for the promotion. This is part of the advertising package. It allows companies to customize their profiles in ways not available to the general public. Companies that have used this method include Adidas, Burger King, and Volkswagen.

While the profile is featured, the company receives lots of traffic from the home page and quickly amasses thousands of friends. Another great thing about these profiles is that MySpace allows them to continue beyond their featured campaign. To inquire about this type of promotion, click Advertise on the bottom of any page for the contact form. Just be sure to have your checkbook ready; you'll need it. Later in the book you'll learn about more cost-effective ways to advertise on MySpace using Google Adwords. In the meantime, you'll want to befriend each featured profile as it appears on the home page to take advantage of their traffic.

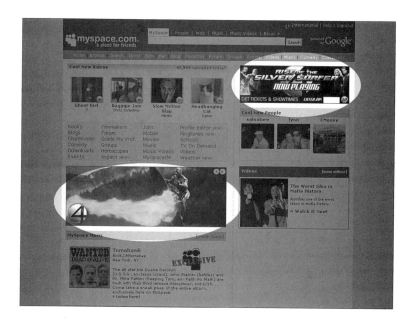

Figure 5.6
Many movies have used a featured profile for marketing on MySpace.

Piggybacking

There are a few ways you can "piggyback" off some of these popular and must-have friends. The first step is to send friend requests to the profiles just described and other low-user-number profiles. It's easy to locate these types of profiles. Simply view someone else's friend network to see who's listed first. You'll also find that many of these users are "loose circle" types, as discussed in the preceding chapter. They will accept a friend request from almost anyone and will gladly add your profile to their ever-growing social network. Once they have confirmed your request, you can begin building a presence on their MySpace page as well. Their profiles represent the best target for this type of work because they receive a large number of page views each day.

Leaving Page Comments

Periodically leave comments on MySpace pages. This can be something as simple as saying hello. If the person allows HTML-based comments, you can include things such as banners and clickable buttons. Be careful with this, however. If a user feels you are abusing his comments section, he can ban you from his network. I recommend leaving only one to five comments each month to avoid annoying the page owner.

Leaving Blog Comments

Leaving comments on a blog post is similar to a leaving a comment on someone's MySpace page. The only difference is that the comments left on a blog post are usually specific to a topic being discussed. These comments are part of a threaded discussion and tend to be more focused than general messages left on a user's profile page. By leaving blog comments on popular MySpace user's blog posts (especially ones that fall in your demographic), you can piggyback some of their success.

Because some of these popular users receive a large number of blog readers, your profile is given a great opportunity to be seen. As you join the conversation, more users will begin to recognize your profile and, in some cases, click through to it. This can help establish your profile (and promotion) as an authority in your scene and most importantly drive traffic to it. To avoid being considered spammy, make sure you are contributing to the conversation and not simply promoting your profile. Establish a repertoire and even reach out to the community; your new friends will thank you.

Showing Your Friends Off

The "Top Friends" section is one of the most prized spots of real estate on a MySpace page. Most members use this page to show off their favorite eight (or sometimes more) friends. Naturally, for your MySpace marketing needs, you'll want to display some relevant profiles here. This can be a bit tricky because if your Top Friends are too appealing, you might lose traffic to them. One option is to set up additional MySpace profiles in line with your main demographic. Be careful, though, because making extra profiles can violate the MySpace terms of service. If possible, fill this section with other members of your company. If you are a band, display individual members' profiles here. You can also hide this section by using the following code. Simply add it to one of the sections in the profile editor to activate the code and hide this box completely:

```
<style>
.friendSpace{display:none!important;}
</style>
```

You can also generate traffic from the "Top Friends" section of other MySpace pages. To do this, simply encourage your existing friends to include your profile in their Top Friends. You'll find that many will be happy to do this. However, if you are not receiving much response to your request, you can add some incentive. In the past I have used everything from giveaways to coupons to entice my friends to respond. Many MySpace users with high friend counts will even sell you a spot in their Top 8. Of course, this may also violate the MySpace terms of service, but it's a great way to give your page additional exposure.

Vertical Friends

You may see the term "vertical" tossed around on the Internet in relation to marketing and industries. A vertical market is a niche market or a small subset of a larger industry. An example is scuba gear. This product is designed for a specific customer and usually isn't purchased by the general public. These types of markets may be small, but they usually have a passionate and loyal following. MySpace marketing can tap into (or even create) the community of users to rally around such a product.

So when I say vertical friends, I'm talking about other MySpace pages that align well with your demographic. Because there is a good chance that people will come across these other pages, it's wise to also have a presence there. How you will find these types of friends is specific to your promotion, but you can easily start by typing a few keywords into the MySpace search box. Once you find a few good pages, browse their friend networks to find similar targets. Send friend requests to anyone you think might be interested in your product or to "loose circle" friends who share similar interests. The next chapter looks at how to expand your reach further through highly targeted friend building.

Precision-Targeting Your Demographic

As we have discussed, MySpace marketing allows you to precision-target your demographic. But what does that mean exactly? Well instead of wasting your time and energy trying to reach out to the millions of MySpace users, your goal should be to focus on building a network of five to ten thousand well-qualified friends. These candidates are most likely to respond to your marketing and offer the best opportunity for returns. They are the people who really get and dig your promotion, your evangelists even.

For many users, MySpace is like an ocean. Giving the right users a life preserver in the form of your page encourages them to latch on and participate. This means they will be better engaged in your promotion, and more likely to help pass on the word. This is really what precision targeting is all about, getting just the right people and making a connection with them. Once the connection is made, we can move on to marketing to them through blogs, bulletins, and much more.

In this chapter, we first talk about who your demographic is, how to find them, and finally how to make a connection with them. We go through some of the common mistakes and powerful techniques used when identifying a promotion's demographic. Next we look at some of the MySpace search tools; here is where we can start to track down the right people. Finally, we learn about how to reach out and build that connection for our MySpace marketing needs. Let's get started with looking closely at our promotions demographic, think you know it already?

Knowing Your Demographic

In my experiences with online marketing, I've found that my initial idea of a promotion's demographic is usually wrong. It might be very close, but chances are it's off just slightly. Sometimes this comes from a misunderstanding of the market or a personal bias. It is also very easy to miss your demographic during the first marketing endeavor you undertake. Looking back on my own experience, it wasn't until the second or third pass of a promotion that I really nailed it.

Thankfully, I've also found that this is somewhat typical of those new to online marketing. Let's face it, most of us MySpace entrepreneurs are, or were at some point, new to marketing in general. After helping hundreds of clients with their online marketing, I've heard just about every line out there. My favorite would have to be when I ask someone who his demographic is and he quickly responds, "Everyone! This is something everyone is going to want!" While I certainly can't fault them for their enthusiasm, it's very rare a promotion can appeal to everyone.

One example of this is a client of mine who sells blind-spot mirrors for cars. He believed his product would appeal to anyone who drives. Naturally he was interested in MySpace marketing because just about every MySpace user of legal age drives a car. It was difficult to make the client understand that although everyone who drives could use a blind-spot mirror, not everyone will want one. That's especially true on MySpace, where many of the users are teenagers who prefer style over safety. In the case of the blind-spot mirrors product, the true demographic was males over the age of 40 who drive a large car or RV. Not a prime target for MySpace, but possible nonetheless.

Another good example of bias in demographic selection is my own. For my niche product of European license plates, I originally believed my demographic was male Audi owners in their late 20s and early 30s. I assumed this because that best describes me, and if I like this product, surely many others like myself would as well. I soon discovered that I was a little off. In fact, my primary demographic was males under 25 who drive Volkswagens. To figure this out, I surveyed my existing customers and then got a closer look at them on MySpace. Because you can look up someone on MySpace using his or her email address, its very easy to get a snapshot of their general demographics and interests. I found that, on average, about 30 percent of my existing customers already had pages. This gave me invaluable insight into my existing customers and helped to fine tune my marketing efforts. Later in this chapter we will see how you can lookup users on MySpace based on their email address and other criteria.

Some of you might already know your demographic in great detail. You've done your research, tested your product in the market, and know exactly who to look for. If this is the case, you are more than ready to get started. The only thing you really need to figure out then is how to apply your existing knowledge to your MySpace marketing. As we go further into finding your demographic on MySpace think of how you can apply these techniques to what you already know about your demographic.

On the other hand, if you have a new product, or your promotion is brand new, take the time to step back and really think about your market. Go out first and get feedback. Don't ask your friends and family; they are more likely to be nice than honest. Give your product away if you have to. If you aren't hitting the right group with your MySpace marketing, trust me, they will let you know. It can be helpful to have as much feedback before getting too deep into MySpace marketing. Learn as much as you can and revisit this chapter several times to find your demographic with what you've learned about them.

Making Friends and Influencing People

A large amount of the friend-building and networking done with MySpace marketing is manually, creating connections one at a time. Although this method takes longer than some automated methods, it helps ensure the quality of your network and is less likely to raise red flags with MySpace. If the system suspects that you are sending spam, your account will be flagged and possibly deleted. This can be determined by how many friend requests you send in a given time. For example, if MySpace detects a user has added 5,000 friends in the last few hours, to them, it's pretty clear some type of automated script is being run. Once discovered, MySpace will remove your account in almost every instance. Instead, with MySpace marketing you want to manually connect with those that might be a good match for your promotion.

How you do this is very similar to how all users create connections—by using the Add to Friends button (see Figure 6.1). This button can be found on every MySpace profile except for those who have chosen to hide it. This feature is really the core of MySpace, the button that connects users with one another and forms a large mesh of social networks.

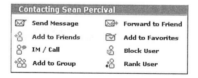

Figure 6.1
The Add to Friends button as seen on most MySpace profiles.

Using this button could not be easier. Simply click it to start the process of adding a friend. The next screen gives you the option to include an introductory message that accompanies your request. This is a great place to let the user know who you are and why you are reaching out to him or her. Typically this is not a good time to convey marketing information. Just write a simple hello and perhaps mention a common interest.

Here's an example:

> Hello, <User Name>,
>
> I was just browsing through profiles and came across yours. I also enjoy <common interest> and thought we should connect. Thanks for your time, and take care.

Replace the text in the brackets to customize your message. Reaching out to people in this way will improve your ratio of accepted requests. Try not to make your introduction read like a marketing message. This tends to turn off users, and they will at best deny your request or, at worst, report your request as spam. If your account receives too many spam reports it can be deleted by MySpace moderators. That of course is the last thing we want for your promotion. If your account is deleted, there is really no easy way to get it back. Because growing a successful MySpace presence takes both time and energy, make sure its not lost over sending inappropriate friend requests. Later in this chapter we cover how to find the right people to send these requests to.

When a fellow MySpace user accepts your friend request, they now belong to your friend network. They will now appear in your friends list and you in theirs. This is one of the best ways to drive traffic to your profile as well. On MySpace, users love to check out who their friends are friends with. So with this type of scenario you get access to the friends of your personal social network as well. Chances are these twice removed friends also have similar interests to the person you just connected with. As you can probably start to see by now, your reach can be exponentially larger by just connecting into the right users on MySpace.

When you form a friend connection with another MySpace user, you also get much greater access to them as well. For example, they will see your bulletin postings and receive additional updates from your profiles activity. You can also view sections of their profile that might be private, things like their blog posts and pictures. Forming these friendships with the right people is the foundation for any MySpace marketing campaign. Now lets learn how we can find the right folks and start to build connections.

Social Searching

Let's start delving into the MySpace user base. We will begin with the MySpace Search tool, shown in Figure 6.2. This section of the website lets you search for a MySpace user based on various criteria, such as name, email, interests, and school attended. To locate the search feature from the MySpace home page you would click Friends, and then Find Friends from the top navigation bar. Next you can enter the information on the person(s) you are searching for.

This way of finding users is more valuable if you have detailed information on your target demographic. The search tool is broken into several parts, each covering different types of user data. They are discussed in the following sections.

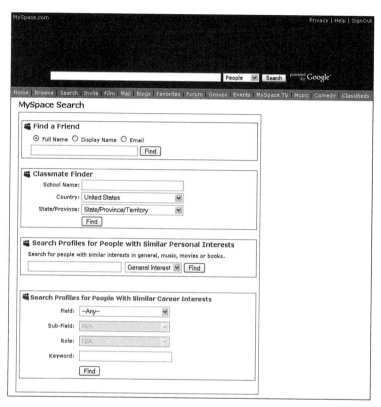

Figure 6.2
The MySpace Search helps you find specific users.

Find a Friend

The first section of the MySpace Search page allows you to find users by their name, display name, or email address. You can enter any of these pieces of information here and find a user that matches your criteria. For each different type of data, you need to select the appropriate radio button above the form itself. When ready, click the Find button to get your results.

For this section you can pull out your old customer databases, business cards, and mailing lists. You should use any source from which you have gathered data about your customers or leads. Using this tool, you have a great opportunity to reconnect and further build relationships. Typically you get the best results here by using an email address to search. An email address is unique to one person, so you will know immediately if you found a match. You can also try using names but you might find that common names return too many results. Searching by display name is not very helpful here, MySpace users tend to use their own unique display names (or handles) that can be tough to search for.

After clicking the Find button you'll be given a set of results. If there are no results, then MySpace was unable to find a direct match to your query. If, however, you do get a few matches, you can view their profile or send a friend request direct from this results page. If you have a prior relationship with the person, it's a good idea to personalize your friend request. Do so by including a message about how you met and how you'd like to stay in touch here on MySpace. Once you've connected with your few old friends and business colleagues, you already have a very engaged audience to market to.

Classmate Finder

To get started, enter the name of a school and a state into the *Find a School* form and click Find. The next screen might ask you to confirm your selection while listing several additional schools in the area. Click on the school name next to See Registered Alumni. This data is pulled directly from users that make this information public. Every MySpace user has the option to include and not include their school history as part of their profile.

The Classmate Finder works especially well if your promotion is locally based or appeals to students. Because high school and college students make up a large part of the MySpace community, this is a great way to find them. Let's say your promotion is for an upcoming music concert. Looking up students in the area is an easy way to get a list of thousands of locals you can market to.

You can also reach out to former alumni to notify them of your latest news and promotions. This works well for those doing personal branding or selling consulting services. Reaching out to former alumni can really help as you might find some former classmates doing similar work. As a word of caution, be careful when contacting former boyfriends and girlfriends from school. MySpace has been well known for connecting (in this case reconnecting) people as more than just friends.

Finally, and perhaps the most valuable, the Classmate Finder will also search vocational schools. For promotions that can appeal to former (or current) attendees, these are great folks to market to. Some examples of vocational school on MySpace include technical schools, cosmetology schools, and various types of mechanical schools.

Similar Personal Interests

The next form, *Search Profiles for People with Similar Personal Interests*, allows you to really narrow things down. Here you can enter both generic and specific keywords. Let's say you want to find MySpace profiles with interests in cars. Simply type "cars" into the field and click the Find button. This will search all MySpace profiles who have listed cars as one of their interests. Try to think of terms that your specific demographic might list on their profiles. Trying different hobbies, bands, and movies related to your promotion is a great place to start.

If you need some more help finding specific keywords try the SEO Tools Keyword Research Tool located at http://tools.seobook.com/keyword-tools/seobook/. Here you can start with one keyword about your demographic and learn about many other related terms. Keep this link bookmarked as it might prove useful with your other marketing efforts.

There is also a drop-down menu that narrows down your search further. For example, you can search only on music, movies, and book related interests. Experiment with different terms here until you get the best results for your promotion. To market a band on MySpace you might find using the drop-down to select Music Interest helps you find similar musical tastes.

Last, when viewing a public MySpace profile you can see the users interests listed on the left-hand side of their profile. Each interest is also hyperlinked allowing you to click through and see more members with the same interest. As you start to connect with your demographic, review what they include in these areas. You can then use their profiles to find additional like-minded folks on MySpace.

Similar Career Interests

If your MySpace marketing centers around making industry connections, the *Search Profiles for People With Similar Career Interests* form is going to be a valuable resource for you. You can search by field for a broad search or narrow your results even further by selecting a subfield and role as well. Social media has proven to be one of the best tools for personal branding and promotion.

Let's say you're a real estate agent, your business and success are going to heavily depend on your industry connection. Use this form to find colleagues both locally and beyond. Become their friend on MySpace and reach out to them with your personal message. Get to know other MySpace members who belong to the same industry. In many cases, you'll find they are also looking to expand their own friend networks.

From my experience using the role pull down menu can sometimes return no results. It seems not many users provide data down to this granular level. Instead I would recommend just picking a field and trying several of the sub-field options. One example would be selection Technology and then Internet to locate web developers on MySpace. Experiment with several types of career searches to find your desired demographic.

Browsing

The Browse Users tool, accessible by clicking Friends and then Browse from the top navigation bar, works similar to MySpace Search with a few additional options. In the Browse Users section, shown in Figure 6.3, you can really drill down to your demographic. Fill out the fields that best describe your demographic by selecting an age range, sex, and even geographic location. This form returns up to 3,000 results at a time, so your goal should be to get down to a more manageable number, like 500. To get the most out of this form, try these helpful tips:

- Sort Results By: This option is located at the bottom of the form and can be adjusted several ways. Using the default Last Login result is great for seeing who was recently active on the site. These users typically are more involved with MySpace and make the best targets. Using the New to MySpace option is helpful for finding users who normally are the most open to accepting friend requests, because typically they are eager to build their friend networks.

- The Advanced Tab: Located in the top-right corner of the form, the Advanced tab is an easily overlooked feature. Here you have even more options for filtering through profiles. If your demographic has very specific requirements, such as marital status, religion, and even lifestyle choices, you'll find them here.

- Location Filtering: One easy way to narrow down results is to enter location information. Here you can select a zip code and profiles within a specific of mileage.

- Photos: Use the Show Only Users Who Have Photos checkbox to help weed out dead or spam profiles. MySpace members who have added at least one image tend to remain active users of the web site.

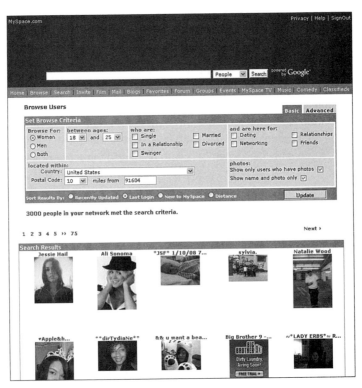

Figure 6.3
The Browse Users section of MySpace and its many options.

Using Groups

MySpace groups are small communities within the web site. Here members can have their own space to discover and share their interests with other members. Each group is given its own unique message and bulletin board system. Additionally, group affiliations are shown on each MySpace profile so members can advertise ones they belong to. Think of them as the modern equivalent of "cliques," a gathering place for like-minded people to collaborate.

MySpace has thousands of groups (see Figure 6.4), ranging from huge fan clubs to little niche communities. Users join these groups to further connect with members who share the same interests, such as a band or sport. Groups are valuable because you can usually find one (or many) that sync up nicely with your demographic. For example, if you are marketing a clothing line, you'll want to look at some of the fashion-based groups, such as the one for "Shopping Addicts."

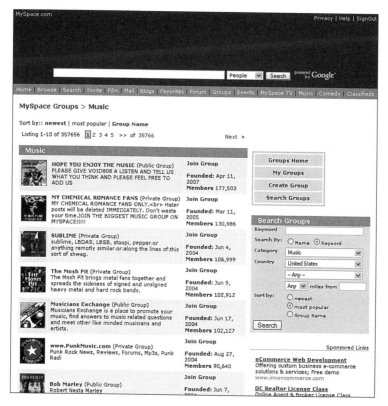

Figure 6.4

MySpace Groups are used by millions of members to connect with others who share a common interest.

There are two types of groups on MySpace, the most common being the public or "open to all" type. Here anyone can join and immediately become a member. These tend to be more common because group owners are looking to build the largest group possible for their topic. However, some prefer a more controlled and intimate group and create what are called private groups.

Private Groups

Many MySpace groups are private and require the group moderator to approve each person who wants to join. These are some of the more valuable groups, because the moderator typically "weeds out" some of the undesirables in an effort to create an active and clean community. For your marketing you'll want to approach these groups with caution. Some may have a no-tolerance policy for any type of promotion, so be sure to read the group's About page to find out. Even if they have such a no-tolerance policy, you can still utilize these groups by getting involved with the community instead of just marketing to it. Join the conversations in the forums and contribute. In return, your profile will still receive click-through traffic.

Public Groups

Naturally the public groups have some of the largest member counts—some in the hundreds of thousands. Because these groups are open to all, you'll want to add yourself to any that match up with your product. The rules here are usually a little looser, so in some cases you can include your promotion directly in forum messages.

Creating Your Own Group

You can also create your own group to help your demographic find you. If possible, don't focus the group on your promotion. Instead, center the group around an interest of your demographic. For example, you are a seller of automotive accessories. Create a group for car enthusiasts where they can group together to discuss their passion. The tighter the niche, the better, because most common topics already have groups associated with them. You'll have plenty of chances to include your advertisements through the various group pages and message boards that come with each group. You also can direct users from your group to your page and, of course, send friend requests to those who join your group.

To get started, click the Create Group link on the left side of the Groups home page. You're presented with a form to fill out, as shown in Figure 6.5.

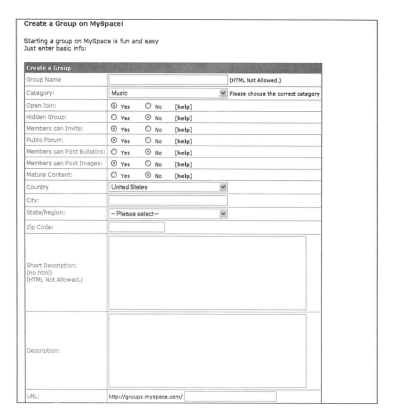

Figure 6.5
MySpace allows anyone to create a group by filling out this simple form.

Keep the following things in mind for each field:

- Group Name: Think of a phrase that describes the interest of the group while keep-ing it simple enough to easily understand. If possible, include some keywords that will come up when users search the Groups directory.

- Category: This determines which section your group is listed in as part of the Groups directory. Be sure to make the most appropriate selection here so that your future members can more easily find you.

- Open Join: Here you decide whether to make membership open to all MySpace users or to require approval before someone enters the group. Because you are looking to build a large group, I recommend leaving this setting on Yes.

- Hidden Group: Used for private groups that do not appear in the directory. For MySpace marketing, this typically is not used.

- Members can Invite: Allows existing members to invite their friends to join the group. Enabling this option is a great way to get a viral following.

- Public Forum: Selecting Yes here allows members to create bulletins in the public forums space of your group. Because you are looking for participation wherever possible, this should be set to Yes.

- Members can Post Bulletins: Similar to the public forums, bulletins appear on the group home page and can be read by MySpace users. I also recommend allowing these while making a point to monitor all content posted to the group. You want to make sure items posted here meet your quality standards and do not contain abuse or spam like material.

- Members can Post Images: Allows existing members to add images to the group. This helps improve interest (MySpace users never seem to get enough images), so I recommend that you set this option to Yes.

- Mature Content: If your group includes adult material, you need to indicate that here. This helps protect minors from being exposed to something they shouldn't see. Remember that nudity in any form is not allowed anywhere on MySpace.

- Country, City, State/Region, Zip Code: This data is used for the group search. You may want to consider using the information of a large city to get a bigger audience for your promotion.

- Short Description, Description: Type a welcoming introduction to potential members in these fields. You can add to these sections after creating your group.

- URL: This last field is important, because it sets the public URL (Web address) for your group. As with the group name, you'll want to include some key words here, but try to keep your URL short and simple. After you've created this address, be sure to include it with your other online and offline marketing materials.

Marketing Your MySpace Profile

Planning Your "Call to Action"

As you begin to drive traffic to your MySpace profile, you also want to consider your call to action. In marketing, a call to action is the next step to your ultimate objective or goal. With MySpace, your call to action can take many forms. You might want to drive a visitor to make a purchase, view your website, or even pick up the phone and call you. Whatever it is, your call to action is going to be that piece of content that makes them do it. To get the best return for your MySpace marketing efforts make sure you deliver your call to action correctly.

In this chapter, we are going to learn how to plan and properly execute a good call to action. We'll take a look at a few examples of other MySpace marketers are using good calls to action. From here we can learn a few tricks that we can apply to your own promotion. Finally, using both image and text links we learn how to drive traffic to your own landing page. This is one of the best uses of MySpace marketing, capturing invaluable information from your visitors that can be used for all types of marketing.

Before we get started, really think about your goals for MySpace marketing. Many start with the assumption that a huge friend network of thousands of friends is the one and only goal. While this can of course help your promotion, don't discount the value of a smaller, yet more loyal, following. These are the people who are really going to get engaged in your offering and answer that all important call to action.

Using Images, Text, and Video for Your Call To Action

To get started with a good call to action, you need to be creative. On MySpace, this means using compelling content to drive the user to the next step. It's up to you to guide them there and it's done with images, text, and video. Each can be used throughout MySpace to drive a user to an external location such as your website or landing page.

MySpace marketers use these various types of content in several different ways. For example, images with clickable links are commonly found directly within a user's profile. Videos can be added to MySpaceTV to drive traffic to your profile and our website. Finally, text based links which can be added to just about any spot on MySpace. Used in conjunction and with the proper messages, these tools help take your MySpace marketing to the next level.

Using Images

On MySpace, images are one of your most effective ways to drive traffic and encourage interaction. Many times, these images are similar to the banner advertisements used across the web. As seen in Figure 7.1, the band Maroon 5 uses several images with unique calls to action on their profile. Each image has a unique message or promotion and when clicked, directs the user to the proper location online. Using images like this is a great way to catch a user's eye and encourage them to click through to learn more.

Figure 7.1
Maroon 5 uses images to direct fans to their official store and several other promotions.

Here for example we see Maroon 5 driving MySpace traffic to several unique Internet web sites. They use this technique to promote their latest DVD, Grammy Award, official store, and even their own custom search engine. While you might not have such a large portfolio to promote, you can get a great idea here of how to promote your own properties from this example. The advertisements are all simple, yet compelling. The perfect combination for attracting new eyes and visitors to your promotions.

For those who have already created banner ads for other promotions, you can immediately start utilizing these on MySpace as well. You can also create your own images specifically for your MySpace marketing needs. Because a MySpace profile gives you more real estate than your typical web promotion, you even have a little more freedom. Once again on the Maroon 5 profile, they have executed this well. These larger-than-usual image ads are very eye-catching and lead the user to click through and learn more.

Figure 7.2
Maroon 5 using the entire profile header (or masthead) to promote their latest album and tour dates.

Using Text Links

Used correctly, text can also be a very powerful call to action. Because the profile itself is already rather busy, you need to focus text-based calls to action in other places. These places include your MySpace blog, bulletins, and even photos you upload.

Text Links and Blogs

Your MySpace blog is going to be your best platform for text promotion. Here, users are looking for a quick update from you, giving them something extra—or in this case, somewhere to click through, which only improves that experience. In Figure 7.3, Maroon 5 uses their blog to announce the latest news and direct visitors to external websites. In this case, they are promoting a new music video and two new items recently added to their merchandise store. We learn more about creating bulletins in Chapter 9, "Generating Buzz with MySpace Blogs."

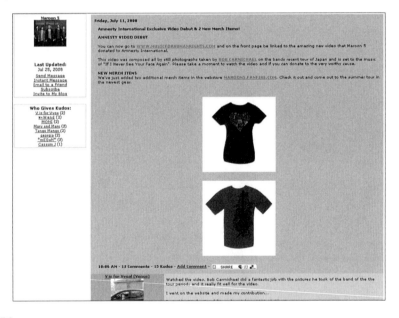

Figure 7.3
To promote a new human rights campaign, Maroon 5 creates blog posts with text links to the official websites.

Text Links and Bulletins

Dropping some simple text links into your MySpace bulletins works very well too. In Figure 7.4, comedian Artie Lange is promoting an upcoming show. At the end of the bulletin, he links to the ticket website, and also provides directions for finding the right tickets. This is a simple but great example of driving action through your bulletins. We go into greater detail about MySpace bulletins in Chapter 10, "Maximizing Bulletins."

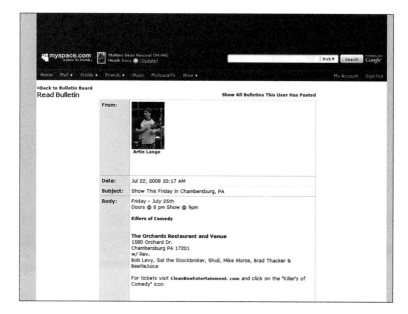

Figure 7.4
Comedian Artie Lange provides links to purchase show tickets directly within his bulletins.

Text Links and Photos

One lesser-known call to action can be done with text links on your photos. Each photo you upload to MySpace has the option to include a caption. Here you can also include simple HTML code, such as active links. As seen in Figure 7.5, the link appears directly under the photo and is clickable.

To create the links, follow these steps:

1. Locate the image to which you want to add the link.
2. Click the Edit Photo button beneath it.
3. Click the Edit link once again at the bottom of the image.
4. Add your HTML code here and anchor text for your link.
5. Click the Save button to confirm the changes.

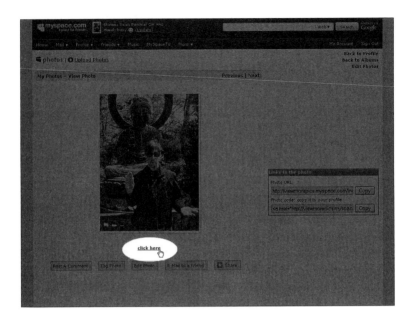

Figure 7.5
Adding a text link to your images is an easy way to drive traffic to your website.

We learned the code for HTML text links in Chapter 4, "Designing Your MySpace Profile." Please note that for this technique your links will only appear active in public view. This means the public will see the link correctly, however when you personally view it you might see the HTML code instead. You can test to be certain everything is working correctly by logging in to MySpace with secondary or friends profile.

About Msplinks.com

You'll notice that any links to external websites are converted to an URL containing msplinks.com. When clicked, they also take the user to an external link alert page before reaching the final destination. This security feature was added in April 2007 to protect its users against scamming and phishing websites. By adding this "middle man," MySpace can better control links added to the website. If a certain URL is being used for questionable means, it can simply be deactivated through msplinks.com. While helping to protect its users, this extra step does hinder some of your efforts.

Using Video

For those with video content, you can also use your videos to create a call to action. In fact, video is quickly becoming one of the best ways to reach audiences and get them engaged in your promotion. One of the more straightforward approaches is to create "teaser" videos. These are short videos that ask the user to visit your website to see the rest. Offering exclusive content (videos they can't see anywhere else) on your website is highly effective as well.

And the end of each video, be sure to include your various website and MySpace profile links. Make sure you leave them on-screen long enough for a viewer to take note of them.

Using Landing Pages

Landing pages (sometimes known as *lead capture pages*) are a simplified version of a website. Within one page, they contain all the information a visitor needs to know. They also can include a call to action such as filling out a form or making a purchase. Long used by marketing with pay-per-click campaigns, landing pages are also great for MySpace marketing.

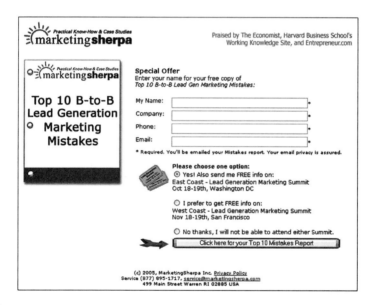

Figure 7.6
A sample landing page created by MarketingSherpa. Visit www.marketingsherpa.com for more information on landing pages and online marketing.

Creating a Landing Page

To create a landing page, you need prior experience (or some help) creating web pages. You also need some experience with graphic design or need to have existing artwork you can use. Because most landing pages are rather simple, though, their creation is also pretty straightforward.

Getting Started

To get started, you need to have an external website where you can create the landing page. This requires access to upload content to your server so it's live on the web. You can set up a unique domain name for your landing page or host it off an external domain. Because you'll be directing traffic here through a few different means, you'll want to keep the URL as simple as possible—for example, use www.yourdomain.com/yourlanding-page/. If you do purchase a domain name for your landing page, use something as simple (and short) as possible. This way, when you include the domain name in images or videos, it's easy for the user to find it online. Once you have the location squared away, you can start creating your page.

Planning Your Page

Take some time to really think through the content for your landing page. Here, you quickly need to provide the user with enough information to make that next step. In marketing circles, this is called the *conversion*—when a visitor switches from viewer to consumer mode. Answer the following questions as quickly as possible:

1. Why are they here?
2. What is the offer or incentive?
3. How can they get started?

You can answer these questions in several different ways, depending on your promotion. To save yourself some time, do some research on what others are doing with landing pages. A few Google searches for "Landing Page Samples" give you a wealth of examples for inspiration.

Capturing Data

A big part of your call to action should include capturing your visitors' contact information. Building a mailing list allows you to reach your viewers outside of MySpace. The occasional email to your list can be great way to remind people you are out there. Today's MySpace users tend to be easily distracted; help keep them in the loop by capturing their email for later marketing purposes.

To get started, you first need the proper code to capture data from a web form. If you ask your website host, they can typically put you in the right direction. Many offer these scripts pre-installed for you as well. One of the more popular (and free) scripts to capture data is pForm from Appnitro. Located at www.phpform.org, this simple website will help you create a lead capture form with just a few clicks. After you customize to your needs, pForm generates the files needed to add to your existing website.

When creating your form, you want to keep this simple, like the rest of your landing page. If you ask for too much information, visitors are less likely to take the time to fill out your form. Start by just capturing names and email addresses. If you plan to do direct mailing, you can also capture this information as well. Just remember that users are much more comfortable giving out their email than their physical address.

Finally, what do you do with this data after you capture it? First of all, no matter how you gather data from your promotion, whether it's on a guest list, contact form, or email, you should store it all in one central location. This can be something as simple as a Microsoft Excel spreadsheet, or something more complex like the customer relationship software Goldmine. This central depository for your contacts should be kept well maintained and organized so it can easy be utilized for future campaigns. If you are collaborating with other colleagues, a solution like Google Docs (docs.google.com) can be an invaluable tool for this.

When planning any call to action for MySpace, first think about a means to an end. Next make sure that end is well defined. In many cases, it's simply creating the connection with another MySpace member. This could be through a simple online friendship or something more concrete. When capturing a viewer, getting their details or making a sale, walk them through the process. Even if your business is chaos behind the scenes (as many new startups are), they should never know it. Think of each connection as a contract, plan for it, and follow it all the way through. Gaining the users trust is sometimes more important than just tricking them to fall for your call to action.

Using Video with MySpace

We live in a different world now as far as video and music are concerned. The family room "boob tube" has been replaced by YouTube. Even the compact disc of today is having trouble keeping up with digital music. Today's wired consumers (especially MySpace users) want media cheap, fast, and in a variety of "snack"-like options. A viral video or music hit in today's market represents a huge opportunity for exposure and, in some cases, a profitable return. Toward the end of 2007, Comscore.com reported that more than 141 million people watched a staggering 10 billion online videos during the month of December alone. Let's take a look at how you can get a piece of this huge audience using MySpace and other valuable websites.

YouTube, WeTube, EveryoneTubes

The leader in the online video space is and has always been YouTube, shown in Figure 8.1. Probably very few people have never stumbled across a popular YouTube video. It could have been from a coworker's email, or perhaps YouTube is already your first stop to watch the latest video everyone is talking about. Copyrighted material aside, there is very little you can't find within the wonderful world of YouTube. How did it get started, and what took it so long?

Figure 8.1
The insanely popular video-sharing website YouTube.

I question its late arrival, because nothing during the first dot-com boom (also known as Web 1.0) even came close to the service that YouTube provides. Previously video was difficult to publish, host, and, of course, find online. The concept of a video-sharing platform was out of reach due to bandwidth costs and the programming required to power such a service. It literally took a tsunami to launch YouTube.

Web 1.0 vs Web 2.0

Web 1.0 and 2.0 are used to define two distinct generations of the Internet. In the beginning, the technology and capabilities of many websites was considered rather limited. Sometime in 2004, a shift in both the technology and usage began to change the landscape. This movement is considered Web 2.0 and focuses heavily on sharing and collaboration between users. MySpace is considered to be a Web 2.0 website due to its many social features.

In December 2004 the world was devastated by the Indian Ocean earthquake that caused more than 250,000 deaths. For the first time, a tragic event on an epic scale was widely captured on video. As tapes made their way to the news networks, they also began to appear online, very similar to what occurs now. However, during this time bloggers were left to host the dramatic footage. The demand for these clips was more than most servers could handle. As videos were posted, they quickly became unavailable as bandwidth was exceeded. This was a frustrating experience for the user, but it was also an opportunity for a new approach to sharing videos online.

Lucky for us, in February of 2005, three PayPal employees launched YouTube and set the very high standard for this type of service. The website was an instant success, and in October of 2006, Google purchased the company for $1.6 billion. The site's traffic continues to grow. With Google behind it, YouTube has been able to add several innovative features.

I Want MySpaceTV

Shortly after YouTube's launch and massive adoption, embedded YouTube videos began appearing throughout MySpace. Users loved how easy it was to post and share their favorite videos with friends. Whether it was a funny video or a music video, MySpace users started viewing millions of YouTube videos every day. Clearly MySpace could benefit from its own video-sharing service—a service that would eventually become MySpace TV (see Figure 8.2). However, this service would not come to be without first enduring some controversy.

Figure 8.2
MySpace's answer to YouTube, MySpaceTV.

"If you look at virtually any Web 2.0 application, whether it's YouTube, whether it's Flickr, whether it's Photobucket or any of the next-generation Web applications, almost all of them are really driven off the back of MySpace."

Peter Chernin
Former MySpace Chief Operating Officer
September 12, 2006

Bullish about its domination as a social networking portal, MySpace made a few strange moves that echo through the preceding quote. On several occasions MySpace took a position that only served to inflame its user base, such as going so far as to block some third-party websites (such as YouTube) from MySpace. The large user base, which was less than thrilled with these actions, in typical social network style organized revolts and protested the blockades. In most cases MySpace reversed its decision and allowed the third-party websites back on MySpace. Later MySpace's tone was very different, as you can see in the following quote from the current COO:

"If you look at the past, companies like Photobucket and YouTube did contribute to the success of MySpace. They were continuing to build on the user experience in ways we were not focused on. Philosophically, we want to make that easier for companies."

Amit Kapur
Current MySpace Chief Operating Officer
February 4, 2008

With a newfound appreciation for its unofficial content partners, MySpace also began expanding its own services. One of these was its own video-sharing platform, called MySpaceTV. The service works very similar to YouTube in that users upload their own videos and then can easily share them with friends. Because MySpaceTV offers some unique integration with other parts of MySpace, it quickly gained traction with users. Now millions are happily uploading their content and gaining huge audiences.

While the videos found on MySpaceTV certainly offer a lot of entertainment value, many have used them for marketing as well. Whether it's a viral video hit or your band's music video, it's a great avenue for marketing. In fact, it's just another location on the massive social network to get your message heard, and in this case, seen. With videos, however, you have a few advantages over other mediums.

For one, your promotion can be dynamic, the content itself is more interesting to the typical MySpace user. Done right, the video can reach well beyond MySpace. Finding its ways onto other video websites, blogs, and message boards, online video is shareable by nature. It's meant to be embedded, emailed, and linked to across the web. Where your MySpace profile can serve as a pit stop for some users, your videos can be the driver to spreading your promotion.

Creating Content

The entry level for creating online video and music has never been easier than it is today. Webcams, simple software, and video-sharing websites have helped inspire millions of online Steven Spielbergs to take to the Web. If you have kids, chances are they figured this out long ago. In fact, kids are some of the biggest contributors. With most computers including video-editing software programs like Apple's iMovie or Microsoft Movie Maker, you may already have the tools you need. Let's start by taking a look at everything you need to get started creating online videos and music.

Cameras

To create video you will of course need some type of camera. This can be something as simple as a small webcam or a larger digital video (DV) cam. Your needs depend on the sophistication of your production and budget. Originally, online video was considered to be very low resolution, this meant just about any camera looked fine. However, today many video sides (including MySpace), are starting to offer their users high definition video hosting. While the quality and uniqueness of your content is probably most important, capturing good video is also very important.

If you are just getting started or have a small budget, look into some of the many webcams offered from Logitech (www.logitech.com). For as little as $40 you can get a simple webcam that attaches to your monitor or desk. These are great for shooting basic videos at the home or office. They are especially useful for video blogging or vlogging. This is where you sit at your desk and speak directly to your camera.

For shooting video away from your desktop you need something a little more portable. For this I recommend *The Flip* (www.theflip.com), a small hand-held video camera from Pure Digital Technologies. For a little more than $100 they offer a few models perfect for shooting video on the go. The camera is light-weight and processes high quality video even for its small price. Its simple interface and easy downloading process make this a perfect match for creating online video.

Overall, most digital video cameras on the market will work just fine with MySpaceTV and YouTube. Generally most online video is shown at a resolution of 320 by 240 pixels and 24 frames per second. You'll want to make sure your camera can create videos slightly higher than these specs. This will help insure your videos retain their quality during the editing process. Upon upload, video sharing sides will automatically downgrade the resolution to their own standards.

Lighting

Lighting is probably one of the most important (and often ignored) components of a good online video. A dark or overexposed video looks terrible and sometimes is downright unwatchable. Take some time to research proper lighting techniques for creating video. Seek help from professionals or experienced friends when possible. For those new to lighting lets get you started by reviewing some of the basics.

First get familiar with the advanced settings on your camera, and adjust them accordingly. Pull the dusty manual out of the closet or look it up on the manufacturer's website. Most video and digital cameras have several settings that can help to improve lighting quality. Get to know how these work and under which lighting conditions they perform the best. Pay close attention to the camera *white balance* setting. Here you find the most control on how much (or how little) light the camera captures.

To prevent shadows you need to deploy what is called three point lighting. First you want to evenly light up the background. This will eliminate shadows on your subjects back and also creates a 3D feel for your videos. Next you need a second or "key light," this should be directly on your subject. Finally you'll need a fill light, called a soft box. This gives the video a natural glow and helps to eliminate any left over shadows.

Research and find the proper gear for budget and production needs. Websites like Pacific Coast Lighting Systems (www.pclightingsystems.com) sell several kits that include everything needed to get started. There are two key pieces of equipment used for video lighting, lets briefly review each of them.

- **Soft box:** A soft box is used to create defused light and reduce shadows on a subject. The box is a soft enclosure or umbrella that surrounds a bulb. By defusing the direct light from the bulb, a soft box creates a natural glow for your videos.

- **Reflector:** A reflector is used to direct light to a subject under low light conditions. Made in the form of umbrellas and flexible sheets, they help control the lighting contrast. They are sometimes referred to as flats or bounce boards.

Video Software

Once you've shot your video you need some way to edit it. For some this can be a difficult set of skills to acquire. Safe to say you won't be adding any Hollywood style effects in the beginning. Keep it simple and learn how to take your video content and filter it down to the very best. If you can wrangle some professional help, talk to them about what types of software they recommend. What software editing application is best for you is going to depend on a few factors, such as operating system used and budget. Let's take a look at a few applications out there available for users of all types.

Windows

Although Microsoft Windows is not known for its graphics and video editing, it does include some nice software to get you started. Most versions of Windows XP and Vista include a program called Windows Movie Maker. For those new to video editing, this is a great place to start. Here you can hone the craft of splicing video and working with scene transitions. Be sure to visit http://www.microsoft.com/windowsxp/using/moviemaker/ for tutorials and advanced techniques.

There is also Video Spin (www.videospin.com) available from Pinnacle software. This free video editor offers many of the same features of Windows Movie Maker plus many it doesn't. Best of all, the interface is kept very simple so the learning curve for getting started is low. With this software, you can easily add titles and transitions and export your video in several different formats.

More-advanced users might want to try a package like Adobe Premier. If Windows Movie Maker is the training wheels of video editing, Adobe Premier is the NASA equivalent. Many professionals use it. The software includes a wealth of editing options and features. Great tools come at a great price. In this case, Premiere retails for about $800. For more information on what's included, visit Adobe's website at http://www.adobe.com/products/premiere/. Be sure to also look into Adobe Premier Elements, this slimed down version offers a simpler interface and lower price tag.

Apple

Apple is well known for its video and graphics capabilities. Included with all Apple computers is iMovie, the powerful but surprisingly easy-to-use video editor. This is the ideal choice for creating high-quality movies. In addition to letting you splice your clips, iMovie includes several professional video effects. You can learn more about iMovie and get the latest version from Apple's website at http://www.apple.com/ilife/imovie/. This product retails at around $80.

For advanced users is a little program called Final Cut Pro. This is the standard video-editing application for professionals worldwide. From Hollywood veterans to indie filmmakers, this is the program to have. The retail price and necessary hardware fall somewhere in the "If you have to ask, you probably can't afford it" price range of $1,300. However, for those who can manage it, this software produces some of the highest-quality videos around. You can learn more about Final Cut Pro on Apple's website at http://www.apple.com/finalcutpro/.

Talent

Finding the right talent for your video content may actually prove to be the most challenging part of producing your own media. If you're lucky, some of your employees might be happy to jump in front of the camera (or stand behind it if *you* prefer to be front and center). Ultimately your videos need to be unique to your product, so it's not a bad idea to include yourself on the video. When possible, try to find a good "mascot" or host for your videos—someone your audience will relate to. Hopefully you'll be able to create several videos and include a nice range of talent. Don't feel limited, though, if it's just you talking to the camera. Many successful video bloggers find great success with this model.

Distributing Content

So your digital masterpiece is ready for prime time. You've edited it to perfection, added your effects, and showcased your promotion. Now you're ready to unleash it and attract the first of your many viewers. Before you get started, you'll want to keep a few things in mind.

Running Time

Typically you'll want to limit the duration of your video to about 5 minutes. Today's online viewing audience tends to have a short attention span; they prefer shorter clips over longer videos. Additionally, some online video services limit the length of clips. During the editing process, be sure to use only the best footage available.

File Size and Format

Online video services like MySpaceTV and YouTube accept several video formats, such as QuickTime and Microsoft Windows Media. MySpaceTV will also automatically adjust your video's resolution and size to its specific standards. This means just about any format or video size will upload and look good on the site. Let's take a look at a few of the options you'll be presented with when exporting your video.

- **Video Format:** If your video editing software supports it, exporting in AVI format is usually the best. This creates an uncompressed and high quality version of your video. Other common options available include DiVX, QuickTime, and Windows Media. Test out a few to find which produces the best video quality.

- **Resolution:** Most online video sites display video at a resolution of 320 pixels by 240 pixels. This means anything higher than that (such as 640x480) will be shrunk to fit. Experiment to see which resolution works best for your videos.

- **Frames Per Second:** By default, most video editing programs offer 30 frames per second as a selection. This setting will work fine with any online video website. By contrast, most televisions and movies display at 24 frames per second.

- **Audio:** To keep audio quality high and file size low, stick with MP3 for the audio format. If offered, use a bit rate of 192kbits/sec or higher. Be sure 16 bit stereo is also selected and frequency of 48 kHz.

Tube Mogul

Tube Mogul is a video distribution website that allows you to easily deploy your video to several websites at once. After creating an account you plug in your login information to various video websites including YouTube and MySpace TV. Once you've uploaded your video you then choose which websites you'd like to distribute it to and launch your campaign. I've found that while most of the video traffic is found on YouTube and MySpace, there are several other valuable video services that Tube Mogul supports. If you're creating this content, it makes sense to cast the widest net possible to find your audience. Tube Mogul also provides amazing analytical data about how well your video performed. Finally they also make it easy to include advertisement directly within your videos. This can help generate revenue to fund your business or even more videos.

Call to Action

To get the most out of your videos, you need to include a call to action. The most commonly used form of this is displaying your website or MySpace page at the end of the video. This is done by adding a text title in your video editing software. Make sure it's shown onscreen long enough for the user to make a note of or remember it. Ensure the font is readable as well as avoiding too many video animations or effects accompanying it.

Better yet, encourage the viewer to visit your website by offering them something more. One technique is to upload "teaser" video clips, a small intro to your full length video. At the end of the clip, display a text message that says "To see the rest of the video visit…" followed by your web site or MySpace profile address.

Another call to action is asking your viewers to send in their own video replies. This helps to give you further exposure as new viewers start to wonder why everyone is talking about. By adding a contest or giveaway as reward for the best video reply you promotion can get a wealth of new viewers. Create a video that peaks the views interest and ends with asking for their own thoughts.

Uploading Content

Every MySpace account includes the ability to upload videos and build your own online channel. For maximum exposure, you'll also want to distribute your video to the other popular online video services. This gives your material a chance to reach an even larger audience and further drive your branding and marketing efforts. YouTube is an obvious and worthwhile start, but other notable sites include Blip.tv, Revver.com, Dailymotion.com, and Viddler.com. Create an account on each website, and be sure to upload new videos to each service. You may find that you prefer one over the other, because each offers something unique. Blip.tv, for example, allows higher-resolution videos. Revver.com can help you earn advertising revenue directly from your videos.

Incorporating Content

After you've uploaded your video (pending a short processing time), you're live! Your video is now available to the millions of MySpace viewers through MySpaceTV. This section of the website is available to all members and even the general public without login. MySpaceTV works very similar to other video services where videos are searchable and a select few are featured on the home page. The featured videos typically are sponsored and beyond the budget of most MySpace marketers. Instead, you'll want to shoot for placement on the Video Charts section of MySpaceTV, where the most popular videos are showcased. You get there by incorporating your video into your profile, website, and beyond.

To get started, you simply need to view the video you just uploaded; you can find it on the My Video tab of MySpaceTV. When viewing a single video, you'll notice several options for promoting your video under the video. It's a good idea to use all of these options for each video, but for now, let's take a look at the most important ones.

Bulletin This, Blog This, and Add to Profile

The Bulletin This, Blog This, and Add to Profile links, shown in Figure 8.3, can help get your video in front of your existing MySpace friends. Each offers a shortcut for including your video within other MySpace services like a bulletin or blog post, and even within your profile. For every new promotional video you upload, be sure to announce it using these links as well. As your friend network gets larger, so does your audience. In Chapter 9, "Generating Buzz with MySpace Blogs" and Chapter 10, "Maximizing Bulletins" we learn more advanced techniques for getting the most out of this feature.

Figure 8.3
You can easily extend your video's reach within your MySpace friend network using these links.

Sharing Is Caring

Under every video and on the left side you'll find a SHARE button (see Figure 8.4). This is where you can promote your video to the rest of the MySpace community and beyond, to millions of Internet users. The button is powered by a service called Add This! (http://www.addthis.com), a free utility that makes use of the many social media websites. In addition to MySpace, these websites cater to millions of Web surfers and allow them to browse and share their favorite locations on the Web. Submitting your video to these websites will bring in more viewers and, in some cases, tidal waves of fresh eyes. Many of these sites use various types of voting systems, so if a video is ranked well enough, it gets very heavy promotion throughout the site. The Add This! service offers promotion to dozens of websites, all of which are a great place to promote your video. However, there are a few you don't want to miss. These are discussed next.

Figure 8.4
The share function on every video allows you to extend your content beyond MySpace.

Del.icio.us (http://del.icio.us)

This certainly is a delicious little website (see Figure 8.5). Here users save their favorite book-marks online instead of to their computer. If you've ever had to switch computers and you lost access to all your favorite bookmarks from your Web browser, you know how frustrating it is. With Delicious, your bookmarks will never be lost, because they are saved online and travel with you. You can also share your favorites with other users of the website. The most popular websites saved on Del.icio.us receive additional promotional on the home page.

Figure 8.5
Popular links showcased on the social bookmarking service Del.icio.us.

Digg (http://www.digg.com)

The mother of all social bookmarking and voting websites, Digg reaches a huge audience of influential Web surfers (see Figure 8.6). Front-page placement on Digg almost always results in 50,000 to 100,000 click-throughs. The demographic that makes up the site is, for the most part, technically savvy young males, so only certain content does well here. Although many viral videos have done reasonably well, anything that appeals to the "geek demographic" tends to have the best shot. When submitting your video, be sure to place it in the video category for the best results. Last, give your submission a good headline and an interesting description. After you've entered the details about your video, click submit to complete the process. Next you'll want to build out your network of Digg friends just like you have on MySpace. Find profiles that share similar interests and send them a friend request. You'll find many are glad to "Digg" your stories if you return the favor for them.

StumbleUpon (http://www.stumbleupon.com)

As its name implies, StumbleUpon allows its users to "stumble" across new and interesting websites picked by the community (see Figure 8.7). Submitting your video here allows users to decide whether they like it and vote accordingly. If your video receives enough positive votes, it makes its way into the stumbling queue for other users to discover.

Figure 8.6
Can you dig it? Digg.com allows users to submit and vote on their favorite Internet links and videos.

Figure 8.7
StumbleUpon gathers the best content on the web, as voted by its millions of users.

Other Social Media Websites

Look through some of the other websites listed by Add This! (http://www.addthis.com; see Figure 8.8) to see if any others would be useful in promoting your product or service. I usually recommend using as many social sharing websites as possible for maximum reach. Each of them offers a unique twist on sharing content, and their user bases have varying demographics. On these websites, take some time to build a friend network, just as you have for your MySpace profile.

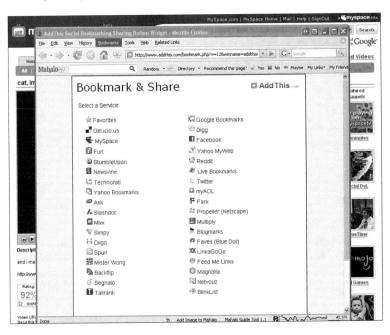

Figure 8.8
Add This! uses some of the many websites that are designed to share content like your MySpace videos.

Generating Buzz with MySpace Blogs

Blogs (or weblogs) as we know them today emerged on the scene sometime in 1994. They were used primarily as digital journals in which authors shared their thoughts and findings from around the Web (see Figure 9.1). In most cases they covered topics like the latest news and updates about the author's cat. However, the focus quickly turned away from felines and toward topics like business and personal branding. Now thousands of people make a living as bloggers, writing about a wide range of niche topics. In fact, most of the most popular blogs today are geared toward a very specific (and highly engaged) audience. Serious revenue can be generated from these blogs, and products featured in the blogosphere tend to get a "make it or break it" result.

To make your specific blog successful you will need a following. Utilizing the wide range of categories offered will help get your blog into the niche you are writing about. The best positioning would be to get into the top ten of the most popular blogs section. This is a new feature MySpace is offering that allows users to access this link directly from their personal blogs. By organizing your blog posts by categories, you can ensure that your target audience will still be able to find you even if you don't make the first page of the most viewed section.

With MySpace blogs you have a chance to create an audience around your promotion and brand. Do it right, and you might give your promotion the "make it" result. Your MySpace blog can also easily tie in with your other MySpace marketing efforts. As your network of friends grows, so does your all-important blog audience. Use your blog to advertise new products or connect with users about related topics. It's easy for a well-written blog to become an authority in a field or with a certain demographic, which can be invaluable for any promotion.

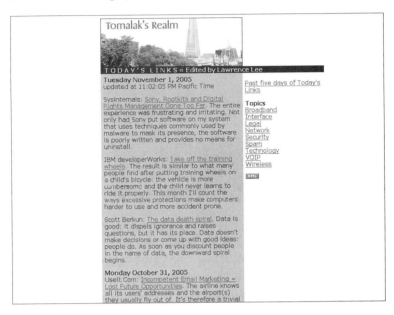

Figure 9.1
Tomalak's Realm, one of the first blogs.

In this chapter, we cover how to use MySpace blogs and get the most out of them. You learn how to write a MySpace blog post and embed various forms of media. We also look at ways you can market your MySpace blog and good general blogging guidelines.

Using MySpace Blogs

One of the great things about MySpace is that it includes a free blog with every account. Everything is already set up and ready to go. All you need to do is kick-start it with your first post. What you choose to write about should be specific to your promotion. However, you should keep in mind a few things when getting started.

Writing

For many, writing compelling content on a consistent basis can be a daunting task. Not everyone is a great writer, but you can become a competent one through practice, focus, and a willingness to learn. Because blogging is casual in nature, it's a great way to learn and develop your writing skills.

Naturally you should avoid mistakes in grammar, spelling, and punctuation. Have fun with it, but make sure your writing gives the proper impression of your product. Consumers will be turned off by typos and poor grammar in a promotion. Double- and triple-check your work, and have someone review your work when possible.

Connect with your audience. Talk with them, not at them. Most visitors will turn to your blog to see what you have to say. Unlike your profile page, this location typically is more personal and information-rich. Share your thoughts while including your promotion, and offer up questions to your readers. Every blog post includes the option for friends to leave a reply, so getting threads of conversations going means you are doing something right.

Learn from the Best

Whatever your niche is, chances are it already has several great blogs covering it. If you don't already read them daily, start. Bookmark them or look into getting an RSS reader. Google offers one that is free at www.google.com/reader. Other notable blog readers include Bloglines (www.bloglines.com) and Netvibes (www.netvibes.com). A RSS reader allows you to subscribe to your favorite blogs and easily keep track of new posts. Think of it as an inbox for your favorite blogs.

Many times you'll find there are blogs out there specific in your field or industry. They tend to be the best resource for the latest goings on in the space. Follow them and you might find they can be the inspiration for your own MySpace blogging. Use websites like Technorati (http://www.technorati.com; see Figure 9.2) to find new blogs to follow and piggyback off of. They give each website an Authority rating which helps to determine a particular blog is.

Figure 9.2
Technorati maintains a popular page that shows the latest trends in blogging.

Prepare Media

Compelling blog posts usually offer more than just text. Today, readers are looking for images, audio, and video that complement the text they're reading. Look for opportunities to incorporate these elements while still staying true to the voice of the blog. Just be careful not to overwhelm the reader with this content. For one it creates a horrible experience for the user. Nothing is worse than having your browser crash because someone embedded 10 videos on a single MySpace page. Use some moderation when planning which media elements to include with your blog posts.

Including an image at the top of every blog post, for example, is a great low impact way to pique readers' interest. Consider using campaign artwork such as banner advertisements and digital flyers whenever possible. To keep things fresh, be sure to periodically switch out the artwork you include.

To find images you can conduct a Google Images (images.google.com) search or browse Flickr (www.flickr.com) for possible images to use. If you are going to use an image from Google they express on their site that they cannot grant you any rights to use the image. The suggestion is for you to contact the site owner to obtain permission. Many bloggers are turning to Flickr to beef up their blogs. Flickr offers images that fall into two categories—non-copyright or creative commons—as it is referred to most often, and copyright or "all rights reserved." You still need permission from the author for all copyright images but creative commons can be used as long as you give the creator attribution. Depending on how you are using the image in your blog, using it legally can be as easy as crediting the author with a link back to their profile. Where ever you decide to use images from ensure that you know the legalities before positing the image to your blog.

How Often Should You Blog?

How often you blog is not as important as how consistently you blog. Writing new blog entries every day can be a difficult pace to maintain. If you don't think you can stick to it, you might find that blogging just once a week may work better. However often you choose to blog, try to stick to a schedule, without huge gaps between posts. If a user clicks through to read your blog and the last post is from three months ago, he is unlikely to return. When a reader sees a steady flow of recent updates, he will be more inclined to check back again in the future or add a subscription to your blog to his RSS aggregator. Finding titles that are catchy is just as important as blogging on a regular schedule. Myspace blogs have the option to title your blog in the subject line. You can also select a category to place the blog in so it is searchable that way as well. There are 27 different categories from religion to HTML that you can choose from. Pick a category that best represents your niche.

Your First Blog Post

You can find your blog by clicking Blogs in the top navigation bar or by visiting http://blog.myspace.com. On your blog home page you'll find options for posting and customization, as shown in Figure 9.3.

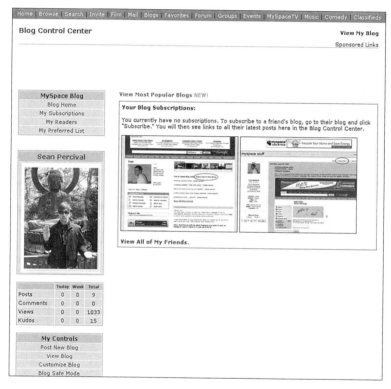

Figure 9.3
Your MySpace blog home will look similar to this. Most of your options are located along the left side.

To get started, simply click the Post New Blog link located in the lower-left corner of the blog home page. You are taken directly to the blog composition window, where you can create your post (see Figure 9.4). Let's take a run through some of the various fields found here.

Figure 9.4
The blog entry screen, where new blog posts are created.

Date and Time

These settings are not very important for MySpace marketing. They allow you to modify the posting date of a blog post if necessary. Normally you'll want to leave these set to the current time of posting. However, you can use this setting to control where a post is displayed in your blogging archives. For example, you might "move up" a past blog post so it displays on the top of your blog because you might have made some updates to the post or its content has become relevant again.

Subject

This field is probably the most important one on this page. Here you type a subject or title for your blog post. Your subject (which is also used as the blog post title) should be as descriptive as possible and also entice the user to want to read your entire post. When readers are searching through the top ten or various categories they only see the subject line or title of the blog. This is your one shot to get the attention of new readers. The title gives the reader an idea of what this blog post is about, so be creative. Try to think about your demographic and what interests them. When possible, offer something unique, such as an announcement or a response to an issue. Also keep in mind that search engines will pick up on this subject line, so include some keywords specific to your campaign as well.

Category

MySpace maintains a huge directory of every public blog post created in the system. The Category field specifies what your blog post is about and how it should be categorized. Typically users don't navigate the directory (there are just too many posts), but they may narrow their searching by category. There are a total of 27 categories to choose from and some that include more than one category grouped together like jobs/work/careers. You can leave the category set to "none" or try to file the post in the appropriate place.

Body

The meat of your blog post is the main content, or the "body." Here is where you include your thoughts and media. You exact content is going to be unique to your promotion however there are a few universal questions you should quickly answer for the reader.

1. Why are they here?
2. What are they discovering?
3. What is the next step?

Always try to start with a paragraph that properly introduces your topic and what you intend to talk about, including the most critical information right up front. The who, what, where, when, and why. If you start off on a rant and don't properly explain your topic, your reader will most likely move on to something else. Blog readers often read only the first paragraph of a blog post, sometimes stopping there or just skimming the remainder of the post. You want your introduction to hook them enough that they'll read your entire post, but failing that, you want your introduction to get them excited to learn more.

Design

The MySpace blog editor includes several options for formatting your text. Try not to go overboard here; use these features only to highlight key information. Your blog should be easy on the eyes and simple to follow for the best effect. The toolbar located just above the text field allows you to make text bold, italic, or underlined, change colors, and several other common word processing features.

Using Links

Getting your network of friends to read your MySpace blog is great, but you may also want to use your blog like a funnel to drive traffic to your website(s). Links to your website can be added to text or images; this can be a very effective method of extending your reach. It's also a great way to provide additional information about the subject by linking to relevant pages such as Wikipedia.

Adding Links Step by Step

1.   Highlight the text you wish to make an active link.

2.   Click the icon that resembles a globe with a small chain link in front of it

3.   A box will pop up and let you enter the URL and the text for the link.

4.   Enter your link (including the http://) and click ok to confirm it.

Including Multimedia

As discussed earlier, images and other media are a great way to enhance a blog post and keep the reader interested. This is especially true with the MySpace crowd, a group that can't seem to get enough media. However, as with your text styling, it's best to use images appropriately. For one thing, some users may have a slower Internet connection, so a blog post full of images may take a long time for them to download. Also, too many images may distract from the message of your post.

To get started, you need to get your images hosted somewhere online. If you have your own website and hosting account, you can simply upload the images there. If you don't have a website, check out the service Photobucket (http://www.photobucket.com), which offers free image hosting. As soon as your image is online, click the icon that resembles a photograph of a tree. You are prompted for the location of your image, which is the full Internet address for the image, for example (http://www.mysite.com/image.jpg). After plugging in this address, click OK to see the image in your new post.

Mood

Although it isn't necessary, the Current Mood option lets your readers know what your mood was when you wrote your blog post. Although this feature is a bit hokey, it offers the reader some additional information about you and your topic. Perhaps you are writing about something exciting, like a new product, and you want to convey that to your readers. For example, if you're offering financial advice, you might use the Current Mood option to convey frustration with the state of a specific market or a recent event.

Comments and Kudos

In this section, there is a box you can select that disables comments and kudos. Comments are important to a blog and should be left on. You want the blog to stay relevant and the best way to maintain that status is with comments. This also allows your marketing to join (or in this case create) conversations around it.

If the feature is enabled, readers can also give your blog post "Kudos." This is simply a voting mechanism that allows them to publicly show their liking of the post. Kudos are displayed on each blog post which links any profile that left one. It can be used as a way to gauge which of your MySpace friends are actively paying attention and enjoying your efforts.

Privacy

The privacy section offers you four different options you can apply to your blog that limits who can read your posts. The public option allows all readers access to your blog. Because your writing will be promotional in nature, you'll probably want to keep it set to Public. Keep in mind that a setting of Public might also mean that search engines can see and catalog this post. If there is something you'd like to keep private or within your circle of friends, you can indicate that preference here by selecting Friends.

Podcast Enclosure

If you are a podcaster (which is like blogging, except in audio format), you can also include a podcast link with each post. These are MP3 files that, like images, must be hosted on a remote location. Using this feature also includes the podcast as part of your blog's RSS feed. For more information on RSS feeds see Using RSS later in this chapter. RSS is a protocol much like HTML that allows websites and services to easily share information such as your MySpace blog posts.

Syndicating and Marketing Your MySpace Blog

A MySpace blog is just like any other blog you find online. This means it can be marketed and syndicated just like the millions of other blogs out there. The purpose of this is to increase the reach of your blog beyond MySpace itself. This can be especially helpful for promotions that need but don't have an official blog setup. Make your MySpace blog your official blog and a destination for anyone (inside or outside MySpace) to get the latest updates.

You can market your MySpace blog in several ways. To begin you can link to it from your existing website and other social network profiles. When we talk about syndicating a

MySpace blog it means repurposing the content for other websites. This is done by using the RSS feed included with every MySpace blog. Next we learn more about what RSS is and how you can get the most out of your MySpace blog.

Gaining MySpace Subscribers

Before we go outside of MySpace, let's take a look at a valuable internal tool. Each user can subscribe to a friend's blog to stay current with new posts. When a user subscribes to your blog, it appears on their personal blog home page, giving them easy access to your posts. You'll notice a Subscribe to this Blog link located on each user's profile that triggers the subscription. Additionally, you can encourage more subscriptions to your blog by including the subscription link in blog posts, bulletins, and elsewhere. The link is as follows:

> http://blog.myspace.com/index.cfm?fuseaction=blog.ConfirmSubscribe&friendID=*XXXX*

You replace the *XXXX* at the end of this address with your unique friend ID. You can find your friend ID number by clicking the Profile button in the top navigation bar. Next look in your address bar to locate the section that says "FriendID=". Mine for example is http://profile.myspace.com/index.cfm?fuseaction=user.viewprofile&friendid=11870004 making my friend id 11870004.

Telling Search Engines About Your Blog

Search engines utilize a program that browses the web and collects information to catalog the pages for better search results. This process is known as crawling. By following the steps below you can let the search engines know about your blog so that they can include them in their crawls of the web. I come across MySpace blog posts all the time when doing Google searches, so it's certainly an effective way of bringing in an outside audience. There are a few ways to accomplish this:

- Link to your blog: Create inbound links to your blog as much as possible. For any related sites, be sure to toss a link and try to reach out to other sites as well for the same. Including text such as "Read Our MySpace Blog" can introduce new visitors to your latest updates and your MySpace profile. Adding these links to your MySpace blog from and external website will help improve their presence and exposure in search engines like Google.

- Submit your blog: All search engines allow you to submit your link for inclusion in their index. In addition to using Google and Yahoo!, look into some of the blog-specific search engines. These include websites such as Technorati (http://www.technorati.com), Bloglines (http://www.bloglines.com), and My Blog Log (http://www.mybloglog.com). Create accounts on these services and go through their process for claiming a blog. In addition to registering your blog with these services for inclusion in their indexes, it will also create a simpler URL you can give your blog readers. Finally it gives users another location online to both find and read your posts.

- Use the proper URLs: Those with search engine marketing experience will already know to keep their links consistent for best effect. Because MySpace is a dynamic website, it tends to generate some rather funky URLs with unnecessary information. Use the following links for submitting to search engines and linking:

HTML link:
http://blog.myspace.com/index.cfm?fuseaction=blog.ListAll&friendID=*XXXX*

RSS link:
http://blog.myspace.com/blog/rss.cfm?friendID=*XXXX*

In both cases be sure to replace the *XXXX* with your unique MySpace friend ID.

- Simple link:

http://blog.myspace.com/YourUsername

When you create your own custom MySpace URL you are also creating a separate link for your blog as well. Following the simple format as seen above, just replace YourUsername with the custom MySpace URL you setup earlier.

Using RSS

RSS (really simple syndication) is a protocol for sharing and accessing blog posts. MySpace blogs automatically create an RSS feed for each of your blog posts as you write them. Users can then use this feed to subscribe to your blog in an RSS reader. Some search engines and other services, in fact, request your RSS feed instead of your blog URL. This is because they can better process and catalog the information.

Although it was only somewhat recently that we began to see RSS used throughout the internet, its development has been underway for many years. Initially created by Netscape in 1999, today the protocol is used by almost every major website and of course millions of blogs. It provides a simple way for internet services to publish and catalog information. Because of this its use has been widely adapted by the blogging community. Users subscribe to a blog's RSS side as you would a newsletter. From a RSS reader a user can then easily read blog headlines and content without evening having to visit the blog itself.

Using FeedBurner

FeedBurner might just be every blogger's best friend—in many cases, a friend you never even knew you had. This free service takes your blog RSS feed and puts it on steroids. It allows weblog owners and podcasters the ability to manage their RSS feeds and track usage of their subscribers. Go to (http://www.feedburner.com) to sign up. After creating an account, you can enter your RSS feed to get started. From there you have a huge selection of available options to extend your blog's reach. One of the most useful is the option for users to get your latest blog posts delivered directly to their inbox. Each time you update your blog, the user receives an email that contains the post and a link to your MySpace profile. FeedBurner also provides statistics on how many people are reading your blog and additional information about them.

Finally, be sure to drill down through your Feedburner to check out the many other options available. In addition to the option to offer your blog as an email newsletter and statistics, you can get even more out of your MySpace blog. Create buttons (called chicklets) that you can use on your MySpace profile and elsewhere. These chicklet buttons make it easier for users to subscribe to your blog in the RSS reader of their choice. You can also republish your content as HTML (for even more search engine optimization) and set up ping services. These ping services notify several major blog directories every time you update your MySpace blog. Tapping into services like Feedburner can help generate buzz outside MySpace, driving users directly to your profile.

Maximizing Bulletins

Myspace Bulletins are an effective way to reach a large amount of people very quickly and easily. While logged in to your account you can create one message with a subject line that gets sent out to your entire network of friends. When used correctly, MySpace bulletins can be some of the best traffic generators for your website or profile page. They are actually some of the most heavily used features of MySpace used for marketing purposes. In this chapter, we discuss what it takes to design an effective MySpace bulletin. We learn how to deploy bulletin campaigns and track their performance. Along the way, a few tips and tricks are included to help your promotion get the most out of MySpace bulletins.

What Are MySpace Bulletins?

MySpace bulletins are a bit similar to a MySpace blog post or email message. Instead of being sent to a user's inbox like an email, they appear on a bulletin wall that is available to anyone in the friend network. They are used as a more public way to interact with friends and share content. This, of course, makes them a great platform for MySpace marketing. In fact, many bulletins sent today are promotional in nature.

One example of using bulletins for marketing is for upcoming events. In Figure 10.1, comedian Artie Lange uses them to promote upcoming radio broadcasts. The bulletin consists of an image, short write-up, and video (not shown here). It also includes links to a MySpace profile and official website. Right here in a quick snack-like format, the viewer gets all the information and, of course, some incentive to click through.

Figure 10.1
Comedian Artie Lange uses MySpace bulletins to advertise upcoming radio events.

Members also use this service heavily for sharing surveys with one another. A simple list of survey questions is started by one person and snowballs through the community. With each reposting, its content is introduced to a whole new crowd of folks. After growing your friend network, you'll notice just how much users engage the bulletins. It's a good idea to pay close attention to what types of bulletins are created by the friends in your network. This will help you cater your efforts to what your community responds to.

Finally, bulletins are a public wall for users to toss up just about anything. Sometimes this includes personal thoughts and updates or, in our case, promotional materials. Their content is "disposable" in nature—here today, gone tomorrow. Keeping this in mind, it's certainly acceptable to set up a schedule for continuous postings. Some do this daily, and others once a week. Find a nice rhythm for your posting frequency and try to stick to it. You might want to keep the subject line of your bulletin fresh. Change it up once in a while so that the reader does not get bored of receiving the same bulletin repeatedly. Whenever possible refresh the content of these bulletins to reflect the latest news and updates about your promotion.

Designing a MySpace Bulletin

Like a blog post, bulletins enable you to include some dynamic content as well. This normally is in the form of images and videos. You might have some of this content already developed; in some cases, you'll want to create it specifically for use in bulletins. Even utilizing some of the basic HTML skills will help make your bulletin pop. Simple adjustments like changing the background color and playing with the font size will make your bulletin more interesting and appealing to your reader.

Bulletins are typically made up of several parts of text copy and several parts of videos or images. Mixed together they create a recipe for the quick to digest format MySpace users respond best to. The content itself should be easy to follow, scannable, and have the user in and out quickly. Include too much text and the users will lose interest, overload the bulletin with images and videos you are likely to annoy the reader. It's a tricky balance of high quality content, and moderation with dynamic elements.

Before we start creating bulletins, however, let's go through our checklist of supplies.

Text Copy

Your exact text content is going to vary depending on use. It should, however, also include one to two paragraphs of well-written copy. As with any text you add to MySpace, run it through a spell checker and get a second set of eyes on it when possible. You want to avoid long blocks of text here, as readers of MySpace bulletins tend to have short attention spans. Keep it very clear, concise, and in a scannable flow. Make sure to highlight key information, such as dates of events or the subject of an announcement. Finally, keep in mind that text loads very quickly in the browser. This gives you an opportunity to learn about the subject while the images and videos begin to load.

Images and Videos

Images and videos are a great way to peak a reader's interest and keep them engaged. I usually recommend the use of one good header image and one video when applicable. Anything more tends to make a bulletin too busy and hard to follow. Images should also be no wider than 480 pixels so they fit correctly in the bulletin. Your images should also be no taller than around 300 pixels as well. Using these image sizes helps to ensure your images doesn't get cut off for a viewer. The area of a webpage that is viewable without the user having to scroll is called "above the fold". It's the most valuable real estate on any web page as it tends to the first (or last) section a user sees. We learn more about how to use images with MySpace in Chapter 4, "Designing Your MySpace Profile."

Videos should be uploaded through a service like MySpaceTV or YouTube. Each include the embed code that can be added to any MySpace bulletin. Simply copy this embed code and paste it directly into your bulletin. For those who are marketing video content, this is a great way to increase video views. In Figure 10.2, my friend Patrick uses bulletins for his online video show. We learn more about using videos with MySpace in Chapter 8, "Using Video with MySpace."

Figure 10.2
Simply posting a video by itself is a great way to market video content and increase views.

Viral Content

Some might already be well familiar with the concept of viral marketing. For those who aren't, *viral marketing* is a technique where a promotion is so well done, it's shared with many friends. The term "viral" comes from the way such content is passed around and its exponential growth of popularity. Viral marketing is a very powerful form of marketing that plays very well in the form of MySpace bulletins.

To better understand what viral content or viral marketing is, try to think back to your own unique experience. It could have taken the form of an email that was forwarded to you, or perhaps a popular online video that you heard of through word of mouth. The key element for any piece of viral content is its uniqueness. If your bulletins offer compelling content you might even create your own viral marketing with them. This occurs when your friends repost your bulletin to their friends. Here your promotion has a great chance to get in front of the eyes of countless users outside your existing network.

One very common example of a viral bulletin are surveys—members fill these out and pass them along to friends to find out their answers. With each repost, the survey reaches an entirely new network of friends and begins to branch out and ripple throughout the

entire site. Creating your own surveys and including links or images related to your promotion is a great tactic. Don't go overboard with your personal inclusion of links and
images though, in this case the more natural and less commercial the survey appears, the
better.

Another example of great viral bulletin content includes the use of a shocking video.
Videos are one of the most common types of viral content available today, due mostly to
their rich media experience. Scan the top videos of the day on YouTube to see what's hot
right now then create bulletins that include these videos and of course some subtle
inclusion of your promotion. Better yet, use MySpace bulletins to promote your own viral
video creations.

Finally, think of how you can encourage your friends to repost your bulletins; in fact,
request they do so in every bulletin post. Create your own surveys, contests, and generally interesting bulletins that users will want to share. Be sure to give them some direction on how to actually repost your bulletin. A user will need to click Reply to Bulletin and
copy the source code that appears on the next screen. They will then need to take this
code and post it into their own new bulletin. Help them by describing this process in the
bottom of your bulletins.

Creating a Bulletin

To start creating your own MySpace bulletins, you have two options. The first is located
on your MySpace dashboard, look in the middle column labeled Friends and then scroll
down to the link labeled Bulletins. This will take you to the Bulletin Board page. Here
you'll find a link for Post Bulletin and Show Bulletins I Have Posted. Clicking Post Bulletin
starts the process, whereas clicking Show All displays all past bulletins you have posted.
Once at the Post Bulletin form, you are ready to create your post, as seen in Figure 10.3.
The second option for accessing myspace bulletins is on your homepage. Scroll down
and look on the left side of the page, where you will see a box that is titled My Mail.
Inside the box is a link that takes you to the page for posting bulletins. From here the
process is the same as when you access this page from the dashboard, although you will
not be able to view past bulletins. You also have a box on your home page titled My
Bulletin Space. This link takes you to the Bulletin Board page and allows you to post a
bulletin, view your friend's bulletins, and view your past bulletins.

Figure 10.3
The Post Bulletin form on MySpace is used to create your bulletins.

Subject

Just like when creating a blog post, the subject is very important here. Users with a lot of friends get tons of bulletins, so you want yours to stand out. This should be relevant to the post content but catchy at the same time. It's OK to deploy some tricks, but don't be misleading in your attempts. Other good techniques include using a question for the subject, like, "What do you guys think of this?" or "Need your feedback, do you like it?."

Body

The body is where the actually content and any dynamic elements are included. Unlike a blog post there is no editor here to simplify the process. In order to format text and include images or video, you need to use some basic HTML. Many of the techniques covered in Chapter 4, can be used here to create an interesting bulletin. Let's revisit some of them and learn how they can be used.

Adding a Header Image

Including an engaging image in the top (or header) of a bulletin is normally recommended. This catches the user's eye and encourages him or her to read through the rest of the content. The recommended size for such an image is no larger than 480 pixels×200 pixels. You can use a taller image if you like, but this requires the user to scroll before seeing your text content.

To include the image itself we use the code we learned about in Chapter 4. Keep in mind your images will need to hosted by someone online to include them in MySpace bulletins. You can use a free photohosting service like Photobucket (www.photobucket.com) to host your images. Once you have the images uploaded and their location, you can include them using the follow code.

Example

```
<img src="http://www.yourwebsite.com/images/filename.jpg">
```

Adding Text Copy

Place your write-up directly below your header image. Keep in mind that you need to format text for line breaks and text justification when needed. Most of your content should be in the standard font; bold tags can also be applied to important text and links. As we learned about in Chapter 4, we can use the following basic codes for formatting our text.

Paragraph Tag

The paragraph tag is used to separate paragraphs. They create a small space between the following line.

Example

```
<p> Enter your text here to create proper space for each paragraph </p>
```

The Div Align Tag

To justify your text to the left, center or right use the div align tag. This courses the text to appear with the justification you specify after align= in the following code.

Example

```
<div align="center">Visiting Our MySpace Page!</div>
```

Bolding Text

To make any text bold simply surround it with both an opening <strong> and closing </strong> tag.

Example

```
<strong>Check This Out!</strong>
```

Including Links

A bulletin is used to educate but also for driving traffic to your profile or web site. Link out whenever possible to things like your official website and content specific to your posting.

Allow Bulletin Comment

Below the body field, there is a checkbox to enable bulletin comments. When checked, they allow your friends to leave comments on your individual postings. These comments are public and can be read by other members in your network. One nice thing about this feature is that you can get a conversation started around the post topic. Of course, this might open up your post to negative feedback as well. I recommend testing this out with your network and monitoring it closely.

Track Performance

MySpace does not allow you to place tracking code on your actual profile. It's a violation of the terms of service and might cause your profile to be deleted. They don't, however, seem to mind if you track things like MySpace bulletins. When you start to roll out your bulletin campaigns, it can be very helpful to track some of its performance. Analyze what works and what doesn't. Adjust your materials and techniques to maximize your marketing returns.

Using a Tracking Service

There are many services that can help you track website traffic and marketing performance. They work by placing a small piece of invisible code within a website that counts each visitor and gathers information about them. In the case of MySpace, this hidden code must be a simple image and not some type of JavaScript code. MySpace actually strips this out, causing the tracker report to have zero results.

MySpaceStats.net

One very nice (and free) tracking service is MySpaceStats.net. They supply you with a unique code that you embed into your profile or bulletins. The code includes an invisible image that does the actual tracking. Because you can generate several codes, you can easily use this service to track multiple types of campaigns.

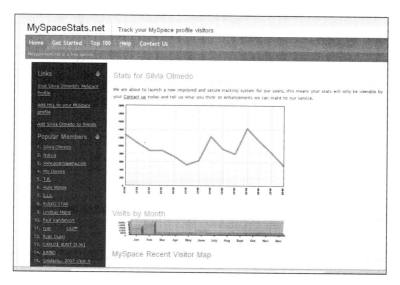

Figure 10.4
MySpaceStats.net can help you track your profiles and bulletin success.

Custom Solutions

If you have your own website and a bit more savvy, you can also roll out some easy cus-tom-tracking solutions. First and foremost, make sure you have some type of analytical software set up on your website. Most web-hosting companies provide this for you with your account. Lately, web professionals have been using the free Google Analytics (www.google.com/analytics/) service more frequently. This web-based reporting package is great for both new marketers and heavy analytical types.

While tracking your bulletin campaigns can be beneficial, it is by no means required. If you are doing it right you'll know it by other means. For a simple metric on how your bul-letins perform, simply watch for the response. See which tactics return replies from oth-ers users and which ones they repost to their own friends. If your campaigns never generate buzz, or even worse, you receive negative feedback, take this into account. Use this experience to retool your bulletins into something that will really hit with your com-munity. Bottom line: have fun with them. Let your passion for the promotion show in the quality of the content you show with MySpace bulletins.

Getting the Word Out with Classifieds

MySpace classifieds allow members to quickly create an ad for a wide variety of topics. They work much like a MySpace bulletin except they are available to view by the public, where a bulletin is only viewable by a member's circle of friends. The classified section is also well organized, separating the ads by things such as employment and for sale items. Every day, thousands of classified are posted to MySpace, now lets learn how you can utilize these types of ads for your own promotion.

In this chapter, we start with the all-important do's and don'ts of using MySpace classifieds. Because classified posts are some of the most heavily monitored services on the website, it's especially important to follow the rules here. Accounts that abuse the classified section for marketing purposes are commonly deleted. Once familiar with the rules and techniques, we will go through the process of creating the actual classified. Finally we review some good practices and general guidelines to follow when creating an classified ad on MySpace.

MySpace classifieds work very much like your traditional newspaper-based classifieds. Members use them for a variety of reasons, such as employment or to sell and buy items. It also works just like the popular classified website Craigslist (www.craigslist.org); however, all posts on MySpace are free (Craigslist charges for a few types of postings). Although it's not one of the most popular spots on MySpace, this section can still be utilized for your marketing needs. As seen in Figure 11.1, these types of ads can be placed to appeal to a very specific demographic—in this case, musicians and actors who might need website design services.

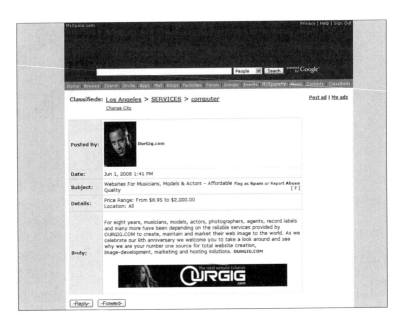

Figure 11.1
An example of using MySpace classifieds to market web design services.

Classified Do's and Don'ts

Having a MySpace account deleted can be a very frustrating experience. After you've put so much time and effort into your marketing, a deleted profile is the same as starting over from scratch. We obviously want to avoid this, so there are a few important rules to follow when creating MySpace classifieds. This section of the website is monitored at all times, and those who break the rules can risk having their posts or, even worse, their entire profiles removed. Make sure you understand the rules and determine if your promotion is a good match for the service before use.

You might want to also set up a second account for posting classified advertisements. This way, if your account is removed, your main profile still remains intact. You may find that classifieds are not right for your promotion and be able to limit the damage this way as well. I wouldn't go over the top and create dozens of additional profiles (MySpace tends to frown on this), but there is nothing wrong with having a few backup accounts.

Test what works and what doesn't, and hone your postings based on your personal experience. Promoting your profile or offering in the classifieds on MySpace is similar to promoting it anywhere else on the site. Track the response you receive (especially if its negative) and make changes where necessary. To help get you started, keep the following dos and don'ts in mind when creating your MySpace classifieds.

General Classified Don'ts

First lets cover the don'ts, these are the sneaky (and I know, sometimes appealing) techniques some have used marketing through MySpace classifieds. These items will almost guarantee your profile is deleted from the site. They should be avoided at all costs. MySpace goes to great lengths to moderate the classifieds and will quickly discover any of the following.

- Post classifieds with deceiving titles
- Post classifieds in the wrong category
- Post the same classified advertisement several times across multiple categories
- Post your classified more than once every 2 weeks
- Include adult content of any type in your classified

General Classified Do's

There are a few standard good practices to use for MySpace bulletins. When creating these classified simply ask yourself, "Am I creating some value here, or am I spamming this service?". Keeping this in mind will normally keep your profile out of trouble and in the end, help you create a better presence on MySpace.

- Post classifieds to the correct categories
- Use a clear, honest and direct subject
- Encourage users to contact your with any questions
- Post your classified under a second backup profile to test response

The MySpace Classified Rules

When you begin the process of creating a classified post, you are immediately presented with the posting rules. It's important to read through these to ensure compliance and avoid potentially having your account deleted. Let's go through each one to clarify what MySpace is looking for here before getting started.

1. Do not post the same ad in multiple categories. Pick one.

There are about a dozen main categories in which you can post your classified. It's important to select the correct one and not post the same ad across multiple categories. If you can't find a good match for a category, your content may not be a good candidate for classified posts. If this is the case, try to think of creative ways you can fit your promotion in somehow. This may be in the form of giving away something in the "Free" category or in the use of the generic "MySpace Friends" section.

2. Do not post the same ad more than once in a 14-day period.

To avoid spamming of the service, MySpace asks that you do not repost your classified more than twice a month. In most cases, classifieds are a one-time posting and should be approached as such. If your classified is a reoccurring item, be sure to avoid posting more than twice a month. Set up a reminder in your calendar to keep you on track here.

How to Set Up Calendar Reminders

MySpace has a built-in calendar that can help you keep a consistent classified posting schedule. To access your calendar, look for the Manage Calendar in the top left corner of your MySpace Dashboard. It appears directly under your default profile image. Here you can easily set up a new calendar item that will remind you every two weeks via MySpace mail or your inbox. Be sure to select Private under the Sharing drop-down menu so your event is not broadcast to your friends.

3. Make sure the content matches the category.

Similar to what we discussed with rule number 1, make sure your post is relevant to the category you're posting in. If you attempt to expand your reach by listing the classified in an improper category, you risk having your post and account deleted.

4. Do not post jokes, foul language, or "adult" content.

The same rules apply throughout MySpace; however, they are heavily enforced in the classified section. The service wouldn't have much value if it was diluted with such content, so avoid this at all costs. Because MySpace has many members under the age of 18, adult content is never a good idea to use in correlation with your MySpace marketing.

5. Don't post ads for "adult" jobs.

Similar classified service Craigslist (www.craiglist.org) has several adult-themed job sections that are unsurprisingly popular. When MySpace refers to "adult" jobs, they are talking about posts for dating, escort, and massage services.

6. Do not post affiliate links to commercial websites.

Oh MySpace, now you are taking away all of the fun, aren't you? So, basically, they don't want people creating classifieds that are simply to promote a website or commercial product. They also don't want posts that simply contain affiliate links. Later in this chapter, we will review some way to get around this restriction.

7. Listings can take up to 10 minutes to display on the classified homepage.

This last rule is mostly a warning to let you know that you may not see your classified appear immediately after posting. Because MySpace is such a large website, it takes some time before your data is made available in the classified section. In other words, don't report your classified advertisement just because you don't see it right away.

Final Warning: If you post anything about Internet money-making opportunities (i.e., get paid to read email, win a Free iPod, and so on), your account WILL BE DELETED.

They put this final warning in red, so you know it's important. Similar to rule number 6, don't post questionable marketing opportunities, such as the many "Win a Free iPod" promotions out there. These types of promotions never get very far on MySpace and should be avoided. In addition to having almost zero credibility, they only further pollute the website and create a bad user experience for MySpace members. If you break some of the other rules, your post may be removed but your account kept intact. However, if you break this final warning, you can almost guarantee your account will be deleted.

Using Classifieds for MySpace Marketing

After reading through the rules, you may already be thinking that the classified section is too restrictive for MySpace marketing. Although using classifieds may not be as effective as something like a blog or bulletin post, they still have value. The usage here may be just a little more specific depending on your promotional needs. The technique is really all in the placement. So, let's go through several categories and how they can be used for your promotion. As shown in Figure 11.2, there are many to choose from for your classified post.

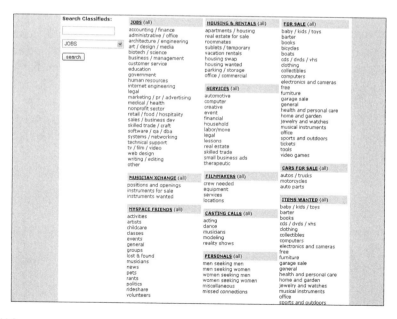

Figure 11.2
The MySpace classified section includes a directory of more than 100 specific categories for your post.

Jobs

This section works great for locating local (or even international) talent for your business. Here you can recruit people to help with various parts of your business, such as marketing, web design, and more. Additionally, if posting ads here using your official MySpace profile, (and not a backup for advertising as mentioned earlier), you give potential hires a chance to check you out before applying. You'll also find there is a large workforce of people out there with various talents, and in need of work. Since many are young entrepreneurs (perhaps like yourself) its very easy to tap into this talent pool for your own promotion. You can even find other experienced MySpace marketers in this category.

Musician Xchange

Musicians can post classifieds about band openings or buying/selling instruments here. In addition to finding new talent for your band, you can network with other local musicians. Here is a great chance to get promotion for your bands and tap into local or other regional markets. Finally you can also read through the current posts to find good bands to send a friend request or message to. If you are a band or artist getting started with MySpace marketing, here is a great forum to meet others in the same boat.

MySpace Friends

This category isn't so much for classifieds but used as a forum for MySpace members. The "Rants" sub-category, for example, literally contains posts of users complaining about various things. This is probably the worst category to try to place a promotion, but it can still be used for networking. Participation here can drive click-through traffic to your profile and incoming friend requests as well. For many finding and befriending as many people possible on MySpace is almost like a job to them. While their traffic might not be the highest quality, finding friends here can help increase your friend network and connect you with other members.

Housing & Rentals

Used to find a new apartment and even purchase property, this category has a sub-section for office and commercial space. Here you can find some local space to set up shop if needed. If you have office or residential space you can offer it for rent here as well.

Services

This category is going to be the most respective to promotions—and even more so if your MySpace marketing is based around providing a service. See if your service fits into one of the dozen sub-sections and place personal classifieds to advertise your service. If your service is not locally based (such as web design), you can post advertisements to several cities. Just make sure not to overdo it; try a new city each month, and stick to ones who are most responsive. I would also recommend doing a few searches for keywords associated with the service you are providing. No doubt you'll find others offering the same and can learn from some of their classified techniques.

Filmmakers

Much like the Musician Xchange, this category is all about helping members in the fields of film and digital video production. Find on-screen talent and upcoming events here or post your own. Posting about your project to the appropriate sub-section helps get your project in front of people in the industry and potential future fans. Request feedback from users on your film and offer a small token of appreciation such as a gift certificate.

For Sale

Here, individuals post items they want to sell in an Internet-based garage sale fashion. This category should not be used to sell products in mass, but can be helpful if you are looking to sell personal or business-related items. Some businesses do get away with marketing their online store or service here, but it's not advisable. A technique that does rather well is offering something under the "Free" sub-category. If your promotion has free materials to accompany it, this is a great way to find lead prospects. Free items can include anything from stickers, t-shirts and more. If you have created "swage" with your promotions logo, this is a great place to give it away and get a few new friends in the process.

Creating a MySpace Classified Post

Creating a classified ad is a rather easy process, similar to posting a bulletin or blog post. Before you get started, make sure you have your classified content ready to go ahead of time. This should include a nice one- to two-paragraph write-up and a single image when appropriate (as seen in Figure 11.3). You may want to prepare the text in your favorite word-processing program to check for spelling and grammatical errors. Once ready, start from the classified homepage, which can be accessed by clicking "More" followed by "Classifieds" from the top navigation menu.

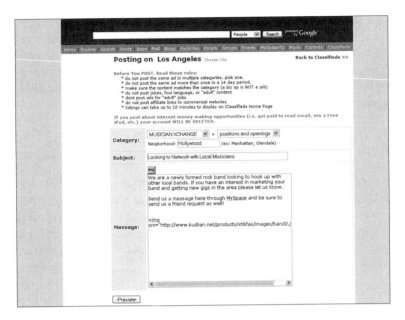

Figure 11.3
A sample classified post used to network with local musicians.

Selecting a Category

After clicking Post an Ad to start the process you'll be asked to select the proper category for your classified. There are about a dozen major categories, with each having several subcategories as well. Take some time to scan through these to find the best match for your needs. It might be a good idea to first look through existing classified posts before creating your own. This way you can get a feel for what type of advertisements are being placed in each category. When you find the proper category, click it to move on to the next step.

Selecting a City

Next you will be asked to confirm your category selection and indicate your zip code. By default, the zip code field is populated with the zip code you have on file with MySpace. Typically you can leave this setting as is unless you wish to target other locations. In this case, simply look up the zip code for that location and enter it here. MySpace offers listing by location so this setting will designate where your classified is placed. When ready, click the Continue button. The next screen will ask you to confirm your location details by selecting a city name close to the zip code entered. Click the Continue button one more time to move on to creating the classified post.

Composing the Ad

Then you will create the actual post by including your text and images. This form is going to be slightly different depending on which category you selected in the pervious steps. For example, placing a classified for an automobile will include fields for make and model. A classified for an event or concert will include fields for price and event date. Let's take a look at the fields available for composing an ad and how best to use them.

Title

The title is probably the most important field on this form. Make sure to craft a subject that is easy to follow and entices a user to click through. Avoid being deceptive with your subject, as this can cause your post to be removed by moderators. Avoid using gimmicky tactics such as special characters or malformed words. Get to your ads point quickly set the proper expectations for a potential viewer.

Description

Now let's discuss the real meat of the classified post: the body or Message field. Input your one- to two-paragraph write-up here. Avoid using complex HTML elements and embeddable videos, as they do not work here. Keep your classified text clear and concise; make sure it speaks your message without being over-commercial. Encourage users to click through to your profile and send you a friend request.

Category-Specific Fields

The next set of form options will vary depending on the type of classified you are listing. A "For Sale" listing, for example, displays a price range, while casting posts enable you to specify desired age ranges. Enter details here specific to your needs. In most cases, these are required fields.

Adding Images

All classifieds include the option of adding images to the post. Currently MySpace will allow you to upload 4 images to the ad. Adding images is done by clicking the Browse button and selecting the file on your local computer. Classifieds with images also receive a small camera icon next to the subject in the listing. This can increase classified views because users know they'll find something more than just a simple write-up.

Previewing and Posting

After you have everything in place, it's time to preview and finalize your post. From the compose screen web page click the Continue button to see how your classified post will look, as seen in Figure 11.4. If any corrections are needed, you have one last chance to edit your post here. At the bottom of the classified preview there is the Edit Ad button. Use this to make any final revisions. If everything looks good, click the Post Ad button to submit your classified ad. After a few minutes, your post will appear in the selected category. Test out different techniques with your classified posts and repeat the ones that work every 2–3 weeks.

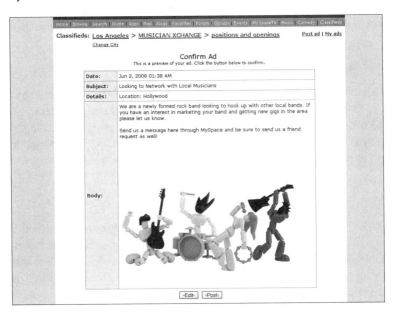

Figure 11.4
The preview screen enables you to see your classified ad before making it live on the site.

After Posting Classified Ads

Once your classified ad is posted to the site you'll want to first look out for any replies. Be sure to respond to every inquiry, even those that are negative. One benefit of these ads is they can help start a conversation between your profile and many other users. Here you can add some valuable feedback about your promotion and make new friend connections. Feel free to send any receptive replies a friend request as well. Adding them to your network gives you more opportunities to engage them further.

Next you'll want to start experimenting with different variations of your classified ads. Try different artwork, titles, and even categories to see which bring the best result. Once again you'll want to limit posting classifieds to one every two weeks. This will be just enough time to try new formats and avoid being considered a classified spammer. Take pointers from what others are doing with this MySpace feature; you'll find they've already figured out many of the best methods already for your classified category of choice. Fine tune your materials and tactics like you do with any marketing campaign.

After placing a few ads, you should quickly discover if classified ads are a good match for your promotion. Either way, be patient while you get started here. Ultimately it should take a few attempts before you find the perfect combination of content and offering. If, however, after a few tries you are not seeing the benefits, or continue to get a wave of negative feedback, MySpace classified ads might not be for you. Don't try to force it, if the negative feedback is greatly outweighing the positive you might be pushing it. Make sure your classifieds are adding to the conversation and not "polluting the river" by being overly promotional for their purpose.

Advanced Techniques

Placing Advertisements on MySpace

U p until now, we have focused primarily on the free and guerilla style of MySpace marketing. Although MySpace is glad to tolerate this to a certain extent, the core of their own business is to generate advertising dollars. You, of course, see this in the many advertisements throughout the site. These advertisements range is both complexity and cost, they can be found on just about any page you visit on the site. So, how can you get your promotion here as well?

In this chapter, we review how to get started purchasing advertisements on MySpace. We cover the various types of advertisements available on MySpace and their associated costs. We look at which type of advertising is best for your promotion and how each type works. Finally we take you through the process and help you launch your first MySpace paid advertisements.

Because some of the paid advertisements on the site are well beyond the budget of many MySpace marketers, we review cost effective solutions available like Google Adwords. Services like this are probably going to be the best match for most MySpace marketers. They allow for the most flexibility in both performance and cost. For just a few dollars you can launch a paid advertising campaign on MySpace today. We'll take you through the process of setting up and launching you first Google Adwords campaign.

Finally we take a look at the future of placing ads on MySpace. Get an exclusive peak at the new MySpace Self Serve advertising platform. It's the latest offering directly from MySpace that allows anyone to cheaply and easily place ads on the site. Although still new, the new platform is going to revolutionize the way marketers tap into the huge audience of MySpace users. If you previously felt purchasing MySpace ads was not right for your promotion or just not cost effective, you might soon change your mind. Placing ads in addition to your other MySpace marketing strategies can greatly increase your return and of course presence on the site.

Placing Advertisements on MySpace Using Google Adwords

First let's go over the advertising option that will appeal to most: using Google Adwords to place advertisements on MySpace. In 2006, MySpace and Google agreed to an advertising partnership valued at roughly $900 million. As part of the deal, Google displays text advertisements throughout the site and within search results generated by MySpace. These ads are typically text-based advertisements, as seen in Figure 12.1. Everyday, Google serves up millions of these text ads to MySpace users, matching the advertisements with relevant text found on the website.

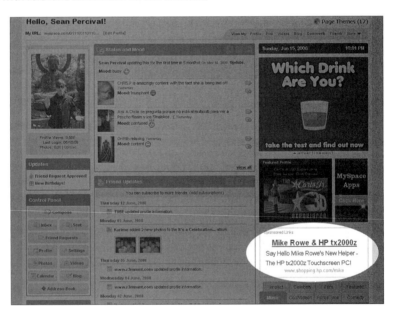

Figure 12.1
Example of a text-based, self-service advertisement, as seen on the MySpace dashboard.

What many users don't know, is that you too can place advertisements the same way. By creating a Google AdWords account, anyone can get started and have their ads online in just a few minutes. The best part about this service is that you easily control just about every part of the campaign. You set the price, where the ads display and which keywords you want to target. Because you also set the daily spending budget, you can keep your advertising costs under control. For anyone new to purchasing online advertisements, it is by far the best service to get started with.

You might even find using Google AdWords to be both fun and challenging. Along with great granular-like control over your campaigns, you get easy to follow statistics to see how it's going. From here you can tweak and refine your campaigns and experiment with new marketing ideas. The program is so great you might even want to use it for non-MySpace related marketing. To learn everything that AdWords has to offer, visit http://adwords.google.com and take the free guided tour. For now, let's learn how we can use the program for placing advertisements on MySpace.

Using Google AdWords

Google AdWords is the main source of revenue for the search engine giant Google. It was here they pioneered the pay-per-click advertising model. A shift away from the image-based web banners of the day, these ads are short one- to two-line blocks of text. They include a title and short description, and display the link of the website. Primarily used for display in Google search results, these are also the links that run along the right-hand site of every search result page. In 2003, Google introduced a new addition to AdWords in the form of site-targeted advertisements.

With this new feature, advertisers could now selectively place advertisements on web-sites of their choice. When MySpace and Google formed a partnership, that deal included access to the millions of members of the popular social network. Now anyone can create a Google AdWords campaign to run right on MySpace. Please note that a valid credit card is required to pay for your advertisements.

If you don't already have an AdWords account, head over to http://adwords.google.com to get started. The sign-up process is very intuitive and helpful. When signing up, make use of the several tutorials and helpful links along the way. You will also be asked if you want to create a campaign right away. You can either create one as a practice or skip this process. Next, we look at how to create campaigns that focuses distribution to MySpace.

Creating a MySpace AdWords Campaign

When logged in to your AdWords account, you'll start at the campaign management sec-tion. Here you can see any running campaigns, including reporting information about their activity. To get started creating advertisements for MySpace, click the placement-tar-geted link, as highlighted in Figure 12.2.

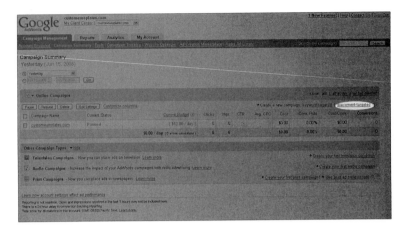

Figure 12.2
Creating a placement-targeted campaign enables you to place text ads on MySpace.

Campaign Setup

The placement-targeted Campaign Setup wizard walks you through the process of creating your advertisements. Follow these quick steps to get your MySpace campaign up and running.

Target Customers Step

The first step enables you to name your campaign and set your customer targeting:

- **Name your campaign**—Enter a descriptive name for your campaign here (something like "MySpace Club Ads").

- **Name your new ad group**—Under each campaign, there are sets of ad groups. These allow campaigns to use multiple advertisements and keyword targeting. Using the club example again, you might call this something like "Flyer 1."

- **Language**—Although MySpace does have several international sites, for this campaign, it's best to focus on English-speaking customers. If your campaign is targeted especially for another language, you can hold down the Control key and select multiple choices here.

- **Location**—The default setting for this is United States. Keep this setting or modify it if your campaign requires it. Click Continue when finished.

Create Ad Step

In the next step, you will set the actual text for your advertisement. As you enter your information, an example will update in real time, as seen in Figure 12.3. Here you want to fit as much info as possible in a concise manner. Use keywords and terms that will catch your demographics' eye whenever possible.

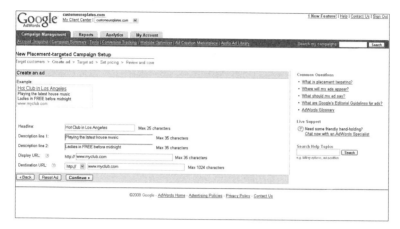

Figure 12.3
The create ad step is used to design your campaign's text content.

- **Headline**—The main piece of the advertisement; add your headline with up to 25 characters maximum. Include at least one major keyword associated with your demographic. Work the keyword into a natural sounding headline for best effect.

- **Description line 1**—Here you have the first line of two for your description. Try to separate two thoughts for each line if possible.

- **Description line 2**—Another field for your description, with a maximum of 35 characters.

- **Display URL**—Enter the website you want to send the visitor to when this link is clicked. Ideally, this is your own personal or business website. You can also link to your MySpace profile as well.

- **Destination URL**—In case you want to send your visitor to a location other than the display URL, you enter it here. This is used for aesthetic reasons for websites with long URLs. It is not meant to be used to trick or misdirect a user. When everything is set, click Continue twice for the next step.

Target Ad Step

This step lets us set which sites to display our advertisements on. Here we can specify MySpace and other relevant websites as well. For now, let's continue creating our MySpace-specific campaign:

- **List URLs**—Click the List URLs radio button to get started. Enter the URL http://www.myspace.com in the box to the right. Click Get Available Placements next.

- **Placements**—After a few seconds, a large list of available placements will appear, as seen in Figure 12.4. Some are based on the location on the website, and others by demographics such as gender and age. Browse this list and select one or more that are a good match for your promotion. If you are just starting out, I recommend limiting your selections. After all, these ads will cost you. Be sure you know what you're purchasing before launching your campaign. When you have made your selections, select Continue at the bottom of the screen.

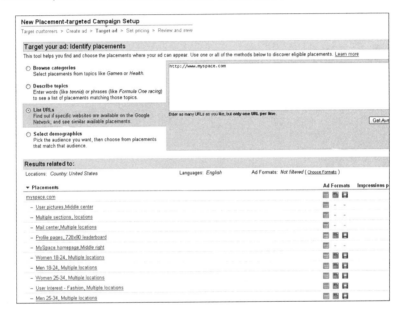

Figure 12.4
Some of the many advertisement placements available on MySpace through Google AdWords.

Set Pricing Step

The final step before confirming your campaign is to select your campaign type and spending limits. You have two choices here: pay-per-click or pay per 1,000 impressions. Both have their own benefits and weaknesses. Google recommends that you try both for a few days and monitor their performance. Depending on your type of campaign, you might find one does better than the other:

- **Pay-Per-Click**—You only pay when someone actually clicks your advertisement. You do not pay for every impression, or when your ad is displayed on the website. This is a good start for those new to online advertising services like AdWords. Selecting this choice and clicking Continue enables you to set your daily budget. It also enables you to select a maximum you want to pay for each click.

- **Pay Per 1,000 Impressions**—With this model, you pay the same price for 1,000 impressions regardless of how many clicks. These follow the traditional ad industry metrics, so this may be easier for those with prior experience. If your ad is misplaced and not presented correctly, you may end up paying a lot for little click-throughs. Like the pay-per-click model, selecting this gives you options for setting your personal budget and pricing.

Review and Save Step

In the final step of the process, you can review your selections and confirm your campaign. Double-check everything here and make changes if needed. Keep in mind that it takes some time and practice to really master Google AdWords. Keep your first campaigns small and watch them closely for a few days. Because everyone's marketing needs are unique, it will take some time to find that perfect groove for your campaign.

Placing Full-Service Advertisements on MySpace

The next type of advertisements available on MySpace is known as full-service advertisements. These are the larger promotions you find in the form of square banner images and featured profiles. In Figure 12.5, we see their placement highlighted on the MySpace dashboard. These are the most expensive types of advertisements offered from MySpace. As such, they are commonly used by larger companies or bought in bulk from third-party ad networks. The price for these types of advertisements can vary dramatically based on where they are placed and how many times they are shown.

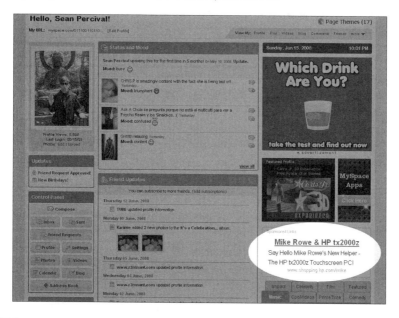

Figure 12.5
An example of full-service advertisements shown on the MySpace dashboard.

They are also called full service because a MySpace advertising representative walks you through the entire process. They will help you get started and even help to design and execute your promotion. As we've talked about already, setting full-service advertising campaigns can be an expensive endeavor—however, for those who can support it, this can be a very profitable one. In 2005, a campaign's minimum was around $5,000 per month; over the years, this number has doubled several times. More recently, the monthly minimums are hovering around $20,000 per month. In some cases, multi-month contracts are also required. Because all this is subject to change at any time, be sure to get information on the latest options early in your planning process.

MySpace makes about $350 million each year by selling advertisements. It's the core of the business and the reason it fetched such a high acquisition price. In 2005, MySpace was acquired by News Corp for a staggering $580 million dollars. Fox Interactive Media (the company who runs MySpace) is banking on the site generating even more revenue in the future. Although full-service advertisements make up the bulk of this revenue, MySpace is starting to expand access for advertisers with small budgets. Service like Google AdWords and their upcoming self service adverting platform may be a better solution for you.

Contacting MySpace Advertising

At the bottom of every page on MySpace, there is a link titled *Advertise*. Clicking this link takes you to the contact form for the MySpace advertising department. Naturally, you would think this is the best way to get started, but sadly it's not. Through my own experience, and when helping clients, I've found this form less than helpful (see Figure 12.6). It seems many of the messages sent here end up in digital purgatory or lost in someone's overflowing Inbox. Although it is still a good idea to use this form, don't be too surprised if you don't get a response. Try filling out the form a few times and make sure you are providing the as much information as possible. When MySpace screens through these requests they will disregard many incomplete applications.

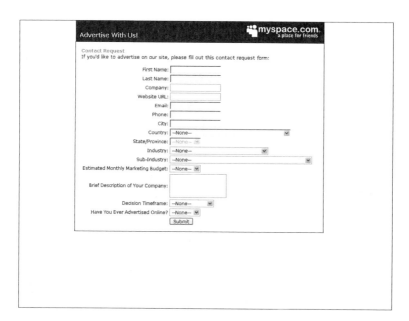

Figure 12.6
The sometimes less-than-useful MySpace advertising contact form.

MySpace Self Serve Advertising Platform

Like many MySpace marketers new and old, you might be looking at both the Google AdWords and full service advertising options and finding yourself somewhere in the middle. You want the flexibility of what Google AdWords offers but the placement that only full service campaigns offer. Lucky for you this solution is now available. Its called the MySpace Self Serve Advertising Platform and its available at http://advertise.myspace.com. For as little as $25 you can launch your own advertising campaign on MySpace that includes not only text, but custom image banners.

For MySpace and it's owner Newscorp, this new platform represents a new way to reach their viewers and of course generate additional revenue. Because the full service system is difficult to manage on a mass scale the new system called "Self-Serve by MySpace" aims to fill a gap in its advertising network. For those who can't afford or don't have the technical ability to roll out large promotions, this new system is going to offer a perfect fit. With it comes a simple and cost effective method for placing your banner ads throughout MySpace.

Getting Started

One great thing about this platform is how easy it is to get started. First get logged into your MySpace account you want to tie your campaign to. Next visit http://advertise. myspace.com to get started. As you can see in Figure 12.7, there is a large "Click here to get started" button, click this to start the process. Next you'll setup and launch your first campaign. Let's take a look at each step now.

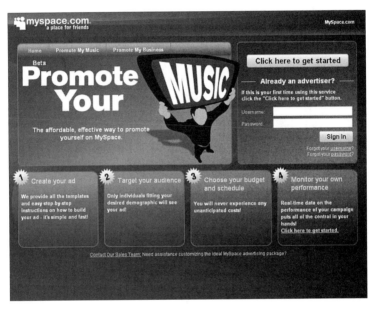

Figure 12.7
The homepage for the MySpace Self Serve Advertising Platform.

Naming Your Campaign

First you'll need to give your campaign a unique name. This helps you track and identify the campaign from within your MySpace account. Be sure to choose something that clearly notes what this campaign includes. As you get further into the platform you may choice to launch several campaigns. By giving them each good name, you'll easily be able to keep track of how each campaign does from the included reporting software.

Building an Advertisement

Next you have two options: build an ad from scratch or upload an existing ad. Let's first take a look at the Build an Ad option. This is great for those without a lot of graphic design experience. Included here are several templates that can be customized to fit your promotion as seen in Figure 12.8. These are available in two sizes, 728x90 pixels (a wide short banner) or 300x250 pixels (a small rectangle banner). You can swap between the two sizes on the left hand side of this first screen. Once you've found a design you like, click it and move on to the next step, designing the actual ad.

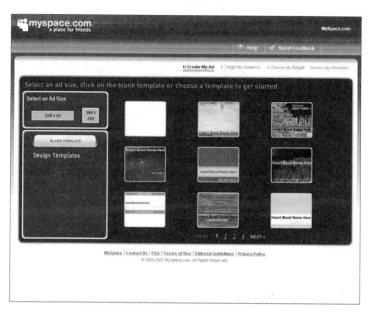

Figure 12.8
Some of the many advertisement templates available from MySpace.

The actual ad builder itself is very straight forward and easy to use. Like most desktop publishing application you simply double click the element you wish to change. Click the each text box to enter your own custom verbiage. The top navigation allows you make all types of adjustments including side, color and font style. If you click the large Images tab on top of the builder you can include additional images as well from your hard drive or MySpace profile. When your ad is ready to go click the Save button in the bottom right corner to move onto the next step.

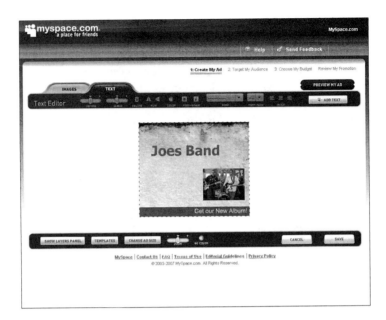

Figure 12.9
The MySpace Self Serve builder allows you quickly create your own advertisements.

Uploading and Existing Ad

If you already have banner advertisements created, you can choose the Upload My Ad option directly from the Self Serve homepage. The next step will ask you to select an image from your hard drive or MySpace Profile. Locate the image you'd like to use and click the Upload button. When the file finishes uploading, you'll be taken to the same builder application available in the previous option Build My Ad. Make any adjustments you like here and click save when ready to move to the next step, targeting your audience.

Targeting Your Audience

On the next step we start to see some of the real power of the self serve platform. Here we can specify the demographic or type of user we want to reach. Let's take a look at each field here and how it will affect your campaign.

- **Destination URL:** Enter the URL or web address you would like to link your advertisement to. When a user clicks your banner they will be sent to this location.

- **Target Audience:** The next box allows us to narrow down who should see this advertisement. You can indicate gender, age, and location preferences and your ads will only be shown to those who meet your criteria.

- **Audience Interests:** Finally, you can select your demographics interests. This information is pulled directly from users MySpace profiles and allows you to match ads with just the right folks. Look through the various interest categories available and click the Add button to the ones that match well with your promotion.

You'll notice that as you set your criteria here a "Total Number of Users" amount is shown on the page. This number represents the total number of MySpace users your ad can be displayed to. If your criteria is too specific, you'll notice this number is smaller. Make your ad open to more ages or interests and you'll notice this number can greatly increase. Try to find just the right balance of general matching and specific targeting for your promotion. Keep in mind you can always launch additional campaigns if you want to offer different demographics unique advertisements. When you are satisfied with your selections here click the Continue button to move on to the next step, setting your budget.

Choosing Your Budget

Next we'll need to set our advertisement budget for this campaign. This helps you control your spending and set your own prices for ads. Also don't forget, you will only pay when someone actually clicks your advertisement and visits your promotion. So even if your ad was to be displayed 1,000 times, you would only pay for any clicks accounted for during those 1,000 impressions. This type of advertising is called "Pay-Per-Click" and is one of the best values for your advertising dollars.

For the MySpace Self Serve Platform, the minimum for any campaign is $25. This means you'll need to purchase at least that amount of clicks for this campaign. If you are just getting started I would also recommend keeping this at $25 until you are more familiar with the platform. Additionally you can always adjust or even create new campaigns at a later time.

You will also be asked to set a "Bid" amount you wish to pay for each click. MySpace will also indicate a minimum price for this as well. Depending on which criteria you selected on the previous step will determine the costs for this. Once again, if you are just starting you might want to go with the lowest suggested bid amount. This way you can test the ad and see how it performs before investing too much of your budget into it. The bid amount is also something that can be adjusted at any time. The basic idea is that the higher the bid amount, the more often your ad will be shown to MySpace users. Test a few different bid prices over the course of the campaign to find the best balance for your promotion.

Finally you'll be asked to set a campaign schedule, both a start and end date for your advertisement. If your promotion is meant for a future date you can indicate this in the Campaign Start field. For advertisements that are time sensitive, you can also enter a date within the Campaign End field. Your advertisement will then stop displaying once this date has passed. When you finish setting your budget, click Continue to move on to the final step, reviewing your promotion.

Reviewing Your Promotion

The last step is to review your promotion and provide your payment information. Make sure to double check each section here to verify everything is correct. If you need to make any adjustments, you can click the Edit link next to each section to make any changes. On this page you should see your banner image, destination URL, audience, and finally the budget and schedule.

MySpace will also ask you to create a new profile to associate with your advertising purchases. This helps to add an additional layer of security to your promotion and protect you from hackers. You'll need to enter a new username and password, answering two security questions, and supply a notification email address to create the new account. Any communication regarding your advertisements will be sent to this address, so be sure it's one you check often.

The final section is where you enter your payment information for this campaign. MySpace currently accepts Visa, MasterCard, and American Express for payment. You will also need to supply the billing address associated with your credit card. Be sure to use the correct address as MySpace will verify this information against your credit card to prevent fraud. Once these fields are filled out, click the checkbox at the bottom of the page that indicates you accept the terms of service. Now click the Submit button to launch your own MySpace Self Serve advertising campaign.

Using the Campaign Manager

After submitting your first campaign it is placed in a "Pending" status. A member of the MySpace advertising team will then review your campaign to ensure it meets their quality standards. You can get a full description of the MySpace editorial guidelines by visiting http://advertise.myspace.com/guidelines.html. If your advertisement does happen to be rejected, a representative will give a reason why and from there you can make the necessary changes and resubmit your advertisement. While you wait for approval however you can start to poke around the Campaign Manager screens. While some sections might be empty while they await data from your campaign, get familiar with what's located here.

Let's go through each of the pages and learn more about what they offer. You can find each of these sections in the top navigation of the advertising platform.

- **Home:** The Home screen displays any recent alerts like new campaigns or status updates. It also displays a campaign performance chart where you can track your ad's impressions and clicks.

- **Campaigns:** Here you can see all your campaigns and several data points for each. Check its current status, your remaining balances and other statistics like ad views and clicks. If you click on the campaign name, you can modify its settings. Please note you will first need to pause your campaign before changes can be made. This option is also available after clicking the campaign's name.

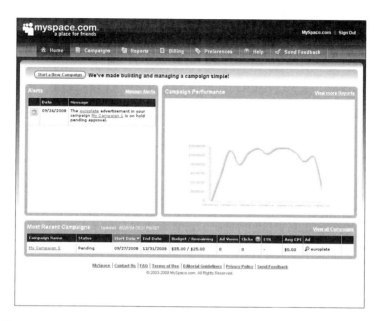

Figure 12.10
The MySpace Self Serve Campaign Manager gives you control over your campaign and access to detailed statistics.

- **Reports:** Get detailed stats about your campaigns performance here. One of the more important pages, these reports offer valuable insights to your campaign. Pay close attention to activity here and adjust your campaign accordingly.

- **Billing:** Adjust you existing billing settings and see any recent transactions to your account. To keep your campaigns active, it's important to always keep a valid credit card on file.

- **Preferences:** Edit your personal settings such as email and password. You can also adjust your email communication settings here as well. I suggest receiving all email alerts at first in case there is an issue with your campaign.

- **Help:** The Help tab is just that, help for using the advertising platform.

- **Send Feedback:** If you have comments or questions about the platform, you can send an email message to the team. Please note that not all inquires will receive a response.

The MySpace Developer Platform

T his chapter discusses the MySpace Developer Platform. This feature enables you to create applications that can be installed by members. These mini applications are very similar to widgets, with a few unique properties. These properties give them an extended reach and real estate throughout MySpace. They can be installed by members of MySpace and included within their profile. The applications can serve several purposes, such as games, or aggregated content from your website such a blog feed.

We go through the history of the platform and touch base on some of the technologies used. Learn how to create your first application, or for the programmer challenged, find some help. MySpace applications are still a rather new concept for MySpace users; it's more than ready to be tapped for MySpace marketing. Because this is considered a very advanced technique of MySpace marketing, this chapter is meant as starter course for those with prior programming experience. However if you don't have this experience, yet still want to take advantage of MySpace Applications you still can. Use this appendix to get an overview of what's involved and learn how to find 3rd party help specializing in this type of service.

About the Developer Platform

In the beginning of 2008, MySpace opened their Developer Platform. This new feature enabled programmers to create applications that run within MySpace profiles. This meant a developer could run more complex code on profiles and connect with various MySpace services. Prior to this, MySpace was heading in the opposite direction in terms of openness. Due to an overwhelming amount of abuse, MySpace had already gone to great lengths to stop many types of code from running on profile pages. The MySpace Developer Platform was created to help ensure that only safe code makes its way to the users.

Competing social network Facebook (www.facebook.com) was actually the first to launch a platform for developers. It was a huge success; with some Facebook applications receiving over 1 million installs. Some developers were even able to capitalize on this success through different means. This began to open the doors for deeper access to social networks. Along with this extended reach, companies began to brand and even monetize their applications.

For the most part, applications created on the platform are for entertainment. They include everything from photo slideshow creators to mini video games you can play with your friends. On the marketing side, some companies have created custom application for music artists and upcoming events. Because MySpace allows application creator to display some advertising or branding, it's a new way to reach and engage your audience.

About Open Social

On November 1, 2007, Google released Open Social. The initiative includes a group of common Application Programming Interfaces (APIs) for social networks. An API is a way for websites to share information with one another. Data such as user activity and profile settings are commons examples of types of information that is shared. Open social and APIs also include standardized ways to access this information and interact with web sites. As more and more social networks are created users are finding themselves belonging to multiple services in many cases. Open Social aims to ease some of the frustration of managing your many social media profiles. It also means you can enjoy great web based applications, no matter which network you find yourself on.

Because of open social developers can create social network applications that run across several different platforms and web sites. MySpace supports Open Social, so applications you develop will be compatible with other websites as well. This can be especially helpful for your business as it helps control development cost, and allows you to reach even larger audiences. When planning your MySpace applications be sure get some additional background on Open Social as well. Some of the many websites that belong to Open Social are Friendster, Yahoo! and Hi5.com.

Open Social makes use of HTML and JavaScript programming languages. It also incorporates the Google Gadgets framework as well. Although it uses many web programming standards, programming for Open Social is still considered an advanced technique. Creating social network applications is going to require a fair level of prior programming experience. For those ready to jump in and give it a try, or just learn bit more, check out these online resources:

- **Open Social Official Site (code.google.com/apis/opensocial/)**—Your best resource for learning more about Open Social. This website includes documentation, code samples, and a wealth of other resources.

- **Open Social Stuff (www.opensocialstuff.com)**—A community for Open Social Developers. On this social network, you can connect with other programmers creating Open Social applications.

- **Open Social Blog (opensocialapis.blogspot.com)**—The official blog of Open Social. Read or subscribe to this website and keep up to date on the latest developments.

Using the Developer Platform

To create MySpace applications you just need an existing MySpace login. Your developer account will be tied directly to this MySpace account. This in mind, it might actually be a good idea to create a new MySpace account for exclusive use with the Developer Platform. In case something happens to your main account or you want to develop applications for several profiles, it can be helpful to store these all under one unique profile. When you have this ready and have accessed the developer site, you can begin to explore the platform.

Getting Started

To get started, visit the Developer Platform homepage located at developer.myspace.com. In Figure A.1, the homepage is displayed, with the latest updates about the Platform. In the top navigation bar, you find links to the various sections of the MySpace Developer Platform. These sections make up the platform and are used to learn about and of course build your MySpace application. Lets take a quick look at what can be found in each section.

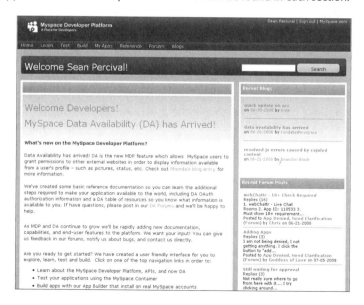

Figure A.1
The MySpace Developers Platform homepage displays the latest updates and a unique navigation bar for using the service.

- **Learn**—The official resource for all things MySpace Developer Platform. Learn about the various pieces of the platform and how they work. Get background information on how to get started.

- **Test**—Here you can test and troubleshoot your latest applications. MySpace provides several tools to ensure that your application works correctly. The last thing you want to do is launch your application and have it fail. Users have little patience for applications that don't work. Test twice, launch once to make sure your application is a hit.

- **Build**—The Build section is where you actually create your applications. Here you provide the basic details about what your application does and include your programming details. You learn more about using the Build tool later in this chapter.

- **My Apps**—MySpace enables developers to create multiple applications that can be managed here. This section is also used to make modifications to existing MySpace applications.

- **Reference**—This section houses all the documentation for the platform and sample code. The "Release Notes" subsection of this page keeps a journal of any code updates made to the platform.

- **Forum**—The Forum is just like the forums found on MySpace. Developers and beginners alike can participate in thread discussions here. New users can ask questions, and experienced users can share knowledge from their own experiences.

- **Blog**—The official MySpace Developer Platform blog is where the latest news and updates are posted.

Creating Your First Application

Aside from the actual programming required to make applications, the process is rather easy to get started with. The Build section of the Developers Platform website is where it all happens. And this is where you create your applications. Because your application is going to be unique to your needs, we can't take you all the way through the development process. We can, however, go through a brief overview of the process and get you started.

Getting Started

To get started you just need to be logged in with an existing MySpace account. You can use your main account or create a new profile specifically for use with the MySpace Developer Platform. The next step is to click *Build* located in the top navigation of the developer website. This takes you to the first setup screen to create a MySpace application. Here you enter the basic information about your application. You will also be creating yet another MySpace profile to associate with this new application. This is required by MySpace and serves to protect the application should something happen to your main profile. For example if you were to remove your profile from the site, the application would still run under the new account you are about to create.

- **Application Title**—Give your application a title; this should be something that clearly explains what the application does. You can also change this at a later time if needed.

- **Email**—You need to supply an email address not used for your existing MySpace account. You might want to consider setting up a free email address for this through a service like Gmail.com or Yahoo! Mail.

- **Password**—You are required to select a secure password for your new MySpace account. This means the password should include both letters and numbers. As a general rule, all your passwords should include a scheme like this. Never use anything that can easily be guessed. Enter the same password again in the following password box for confirmation.

- **Terms of Use**—To use the MySpace Developer Platform, you need to agree to their terms of use. The terms include information on proper use of the platform and MySpace in general. Read through this information and click the check box to confirm.

Once you have filled out the fields, click the Next button to continue. On the following screen, you will be asked to pass a CAPTCHA test, as seen in Figure A.2. This step is to avoid developers from automating the signup process.

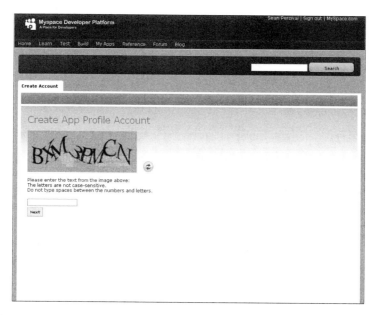

Figure A.2
CAPTHCA helps to avoid automated scripts from creating applications. Enter the code you see here; you can also use the arrows to the right of the letter to generate a new code. If you can not read the text here use the arrows button to get a new code.

Uploading an Application XML File

The following screen gives you the option to upload your application's XML file. An XML file is an open standard file type that easily exports and imports data into various web services. As seen in Figure A.3, this is primarily for developers who have already created a social network application that is compatible with MySpace. Here, an XML file can be used to easily port your application settings right into MySpace. Information such as title, description, and thumbnail images can all be set here.

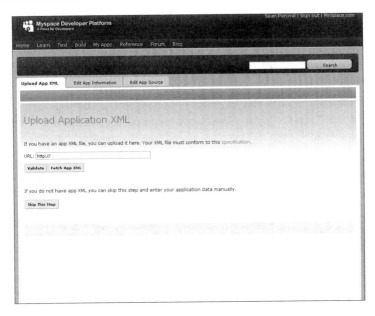

Figure A.3
Import existing application XML files here for use with the MySpace Developers Platform.

If you are new to the MySpace Developer Platform, and don't have an existing XML file, you can use the Skip This Step button at the bottom of the page to advance to the next step. On the following screen, you get the option to manually enter all your MySpace application information. For those just experimenting with the service, you'll probably want to skip this step all together.

Those with existing application XML files should first verify that their file confirms to proper specifications. The MySpace Developers Platform conforms to the Gadget XSD protocol and uses many of the same attributes. You can learn more about this protocol online at http://opensocial-resources.googlecode.com/svn/spec/0.8/gadgets/gadgets-extended.xsd

Using the MySpace Application Builder

The next step takes you directly into the MySpace Application builder. Here, you have three tabs on the top for creating your application. The Upload App XML tab takes you back to the previous step. You can upload an XML or update an existing one. The Edit App Information tab is used to enter the basic details of your application. Finally, the Edit App Source enables you to include the actual source code for your application. Let's take a look at each section now.

Upload App XML

Here you can upload an XML file for your application. You can also update an existing one if you've made changes to your settings offline. This file contains data specific to your application and is used to transfer application settings from one platform to another.

Edit App Information

Here we enter all the basic information about the application and indicate some basic settings. The Main App Settings box information is used for the Application Directory and seen by anyone who installs your application.

Edit App Source

The App Source tab is used to store the code for your application. Because a MySpace application appears in several locations on the site, you have options for each layout here.

Finding Help with Creating Your Application

If this technique is starting to get a little more technical than you are comfortable with, don't worry. There are plenty of developers and even companies now that specialize in creating social network applications. Let's look at a few resources for finding that rock star developer who can turn your application dreams into a reality.

The Developer Forums

The official MySpace developer forums can be found at developer.myspace.com/community/forums/. Here you can connect with other members developing MySpace applications. You can pose your own questions here and start a new threaded discussion. Fellow MySpace developers are usually glad to help if you run into any problems with your applications. It's also a good idea to answer questions from other members if you have some experience with the issue. This helps build trust within the developer community and offers networking opportunities for your applications.

It's also a good place to locate developers who can create a MySpace application for you. Take some time to browse through the message board threads to locate experiences developers. By clicking their user name you can visit their profile to learn more about them or see applications they have developed. You might want to avoid any actual recruiting on the public forms. Instead, send them a private MySpace email to get started. While MySpace will tolerate this to a small extent its better to keep these discussions in a private manner.

Finding Local Talent

Sometimes it's best to find a local company or consultant who can help you. This way, you can meet face to face to discuss and plan your application needs. Because social network applications have become rather popular recently, you'll find there is a good chance to locate a developer in your area. Let's take a look at a few ways to find local developers for your MySpace applications.

Craigslist (www.craigslist.org)

Craiglist is a popular message and job board that started in San Francisco, California. They now have specialized sites for just about every major metropolitan area across America. Visit the site and locate the closest city to your home town and click it. Next click the *web / info design* link located under the *Jobs* category. Finally, click the *Post Ad* link in top right corner of the page. Here you can create your own job posting and indicate the type of help you are looking for. Let them know you seek someone with prior experience developing MySpace applications or creating Open Social based social applications.

LinkedIn (www.linkedin.com)

LinkedIn is a social network for executives and consultants. It includes about 25 millions members from all types of industries. Tech savvy consultants and applications developers are especially fond of LinkedIn for its ability to network with new clients. If you haven't already, create a profile for yourself and begin search for MySpace developers in your area. Use the search and advanced search tools to narrow your results to your local area.

Barcamp (www.barcamp.org)

Barcamp is a new type of conference that allows local developers and technology enthusiasts to network and collaborate. Put on across the country, these free conferences can be one of the best ways to meet the rock star developers in your area. Visit the official site to look up upcoming events around you. Next its as simple as attending the event (they are all free) and start meeting your future development team.

Using Application Development Companies

As social media applications have started to become more popular, several companies have launched to provide service and support in the area. You can conduct a few Google searches on the topic to start your research. I also recommend making contact with Context (www.contextoptional.com), a company that specializes in social network application design.

Index

MySpace profiles. *See also* friend profiles
creating, 35, 37
custom URL, selecting, 43-44
email verification process, 42-43
Invite page, 41-42
MySpace Dashboard, 41-47
photos, adding to profile, 40-41
signup form, 38-40
designing, 49-50
CSS usage, 56
free images/layouts, finding, 62-63
future of, 67
HTML usage, 51-55
images in, 56-58
music, adding, 63-65
options for, 50-51
with profile editors, 58-62
video, adding, 65-66
featured profiles, 78-79
incorporating videos in, 115-116
separating personal and business profiles, 36
Tom Anderson, 31
types of, 36-37
user profile numbers, 78
MySpace Self Serve Advertising Platform, 165-166
building ads with, 166-168
Campaign Manager screens, 170-171
naming ad campaigns, 166

reviewing the promotion, 170
selecting the budget, 169
targeting the audience, 168-169
uploading existing ads, 168
MySpaceStats.net, 140-141
MySpaceTV, 65-66
origin of, 109-110
Video Charts section, 116

N

name (on signup form), 38
naming ad campaigns, 166
negative feedback, preparing for, 22
Netvibes, 123
Nguyen, Tila. *See* Tila Tequila example
niche products/services, MySpace marketing of, 13-14, 84-85
nodes in social networks, 11-12

O

on-screen talent for video, 113
online communities. *See* social networks
online gambling, 75
online resources for HTML help, 52
online retail websites, MySpace marketing by, 12-13
online videos. *See* videos
Open Social, overview, 174-175

Open Social Blog website, 175
Open Social Official Site website, 174
Open Social Stuff website, 175

P

p tag (HTML), 54
Pacific Coast Lighting Systems, 112
page comments, posting, 79
pages. *See* MySpace profiles
paid advertisements, 9, 157-158
contacting MySpace advertising depart-ment, 164-165
cost of, 2
featured profiles, 78-79
full-service advertise-ments, 163-164
with Google AdWords, 158-159
Campaign Setup wizard, 159-163
self-serve advertising platform, 165-166
building ads with, 166-168
Campaign Manager screens, 170-171
naming ad campaigns, 166
reviewing the promotion, 170
selecting the budget, 169
targeting the audience, 168-169
uploading existing ads, 168

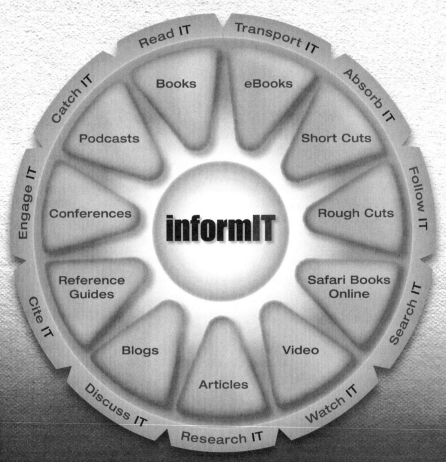

FREE Online Edition

Your purchase of *MySpace® Marketing: Creating a Social Network to Boom Your Business* includes access to a free online edition for 45 days through the Safari Books Online subscription service. Nearly every Que book is available online through Safari Books Online, along with more than 5,000 other technical books and videos from publishers such as Addison-Wesley Professional, Cisco Press, Exam Cram, IBM Press, O'Reilly, Prentice Hall, and Sams.

SAFARI BOOKS ONLINE allows you to search for a specific answer, cut and paste code, download chapters, and stay current with emerging technologies.

Activate your FREE Online Edition at
www.informit.com/safarifree

STEP 1: Enter the coupon code: FLDLRFA.

STEP 2: New Safari users, complete the brief registration form. Safari subscribers, just log in.

If you have difficulty registering on Safari or accessing the online edition, please e-mail customer-service@safaribooksonline.com